Special Edition of the

The Colloquium for Information System Security Education (CISSE)

A Study of State Cybersecurity Capabilities for Local and Regional Collaboration

February, 2016

CISSE Edition 3, Issue 2

The Colloquium for Information Systems Security Education (CISSE), USA Non-Profit Corporation.

Please contact us at *askCISSE@cisse.info*

www.cisse.info

Text Copyright © 2016

Table of Contents

Editor's Comments..iv

Cyber Public Private Partnership ICS/SCADA and Critical Infrastructure Protection Strategic Vision 7

    Executive Summary... 7

    Conclusions / Recommendations 8

    Background 9

    Discussion..11

    Program Purpose 15

    Program Objectives 19

    Table of State by State Cybersecurity Capabilities....................21

    Conclusions 50

    Bibliography 52

Appendix: State by State Detailed Reports..54

    Alabama..54

    Alaska 59

    Arizona...61

    Arkansas 66

    California..69

    Colorado 77

    Connecticut..83

    District of Columbia 86

    Delaware 91

    Florida..96

    Georgia...104

    Hawaii...110

Idaho	115
Illinois	118
Indiana	124
Iowa	126
Kansas	129
Kentucy	133
Louisiana	135
Maine	137
Maryland	139
Massachusetts	147
Michigan	153
Minnesota	157
Mississippi	160
Missouri	162
Montana	164
Nebraska	167
Nevada	171
New Hampshire	178
New Jersey	181
New Mexico	185
New York	189
North Carolina	193
North Dakota	199
Ohio	202
Oklahoma	206
Oregon	209

Pennsylvania 221

Rhode Island 228

South Carolina 230

South Dakota 232

Tennessee 234

Texas 236

Utah 248

Vermont 252

Virginia 254

Washington 258

West Virginia 263

Wisconsin 266

Wyoming 270

Editor's Comments

From the beginning, cross-sector collaboration—academia, government, industry—has been the hallmark of The Colloquium for Information Systems Security Education (CISSE) and is enshrined in its logo. Begun as the National Colloquium for Information Systems Security Education (NCISSE) in 1996, the organization was founded to provide a forum for cybersecurity dialogue among leaders from government, industry, and academia. In June 2002, NCISSE became The Colloquium for Information Systems Security Education (CISSE) or more simply--The Colloquium—when its mission expanded to include international participation.

While the focus of CISSE in the United States has been at the Federal level, providing support for educators, endorsing national curriculum standards, sharing best practices, encouraging the creation of NSA/DHS Centers for Academic Excellence (CAEs) in Information Assurance Education (CAE-IAD) and Research (CAE-R), there is an expanding role for CISSE emerging at the state and local level. Recently, this has been reflected in the development of cross-sector collaborations within states and regions for cyber incident preparedness and response.

In the event of a catastrophic event that would disrupt Internet-connected critical infrastructure, the effects will be felt locally and the response, likewise, will be at the local level, in collaboration with the appropriate Federal agencies. In this endeavor, academic institutions offer a neutral environment to convene the appropriate cross-sector participants who can plan for preparedness and assume roles in the event of a necessary response.

Example: Regional Economic Cyber Analysis Platform (RECAP) in Washington State

An example of a successful state-wide, cross-sector collaboration is the Regional Economic Cyber Analysis Platform (RECAP) (aka Public Regional Information Security Event Management, or PRISEM). This is a unique DHS-funded service which aggregates and processes cybersecurity alerts and extends cyber situational awareness over the greater Puget Sound area. RECAP is an operational partnership among the City of Seattle, the University of Washington's Center for Information Assurance and Cybersecurity (CIAC), a CAE-IAD and CAE-R, and the Dept. of Homeland Security, along with local governments, maritime ports and several local and public organizations that manage critical infrastructure systems.

While these local institutions are not resourced for the type of monitoring that detects modern attacks, impacts they sustain from cyberattack will have significant effects on the regional economy as a whole, as well as the Nation. This was the motivation for creating RECAP. In a proof-of-concept, RECAP has achieved real-time, cross-organizational, cross-sector data sharing, overcoming the legal impediments that make such sharing so difficult. RECAP collaborators are now mentoring replication to other regions, working with several states to establish similar collaborations that are being adapted to reflect the unique local institutions in each.

In each instance of replication, the local academic institutions provide a key forum for convening the proposed participants. Receptivity of each potential state to re-creating such a capability is correlated to the cyber awareness and readiness of each state and the availability of an interested and well-established CAE. For that reason, the editors of this volume have aggregated data reflecting the CAEs and cyber-readiness of each state in order to serve as a guide for those implementing this and similar local projects. CISSE, as the publisher of this information, is embracing local preparedness as an expansion of the services they can provide its membership of over 200 academic institutions.

A white paper entitled: Cyber Public Private Partnership ICS/SCADA and Critical Infrastructure Protection Strategic Vision follows that describes insight into a project spawned from RECAP. It's shared as an example of the types of projects that may be possible in your state or region. The table by state describes resources within your state that could be deployed on your projects.

Please note: It is the intent of the CISSE editors to update this volume on a regular basis and encourages its CAE membership to review information on their, respective, states/CAEs reflected in this volume and offer updates, corrections and further insights.

Editor of this Special Edition of CISSE Journal

Barbara Endicott-Popovsky, Ph.D.
Professor University of Washington Institute of Technology
Executive Director, Center for Information Assurance and Cybersecurity

With:

Volodymyr Lysenko, Ph.D.
Post-Doctoral Research Assistant
Center for Information Assurance and Cybersecurity

Assisted by:

Justin Brecese, *SFS Student*
Casey Rodgers, *SFS Student*
Morgan Zantua, *Architect – Cyber4Vets*

Copy Editing for Publication by:

Daniel Shoemaker, Ph.D. and Tamara Shoemaker on behalf of CISSE

Cyber Public Private Partnership ICS/SCADA and Critical Infrastructure Protection Strategic Vision

Col. Scott Nelson

Dr. Barbara Endicott-Popovsky

EXECUTIVE SUMMARY

Since 2003 cyberspace has become a significant national asset for the United States and our elements of national power: Diplomacy, Informational, Military and Economic (DIME). The global balance of power is now shaped by a new multi-polar diffusion of power, disruptive technologies and Moore's law of technology advancement [1]. These factors have enabled cyberspace Advanced Persistent Threats (APT) which include; criminal networks, nation states, terrorist organizations and others, to develop leveling strategies against the United States national strengths; however, early in the Internet's development the focus was on access and ease of connection, not security. Cyberspace today now hosts and underwrites the global economic market worth trillions of dollars. The United States is critically unprepared for a massive disruption of our critical infrastructure from a cyberattack. APTs (Nation states and non-state actors) have identified and continue to map critical vulnerabilities in each of our national critical infrastructure sectors: chemical, communications, commercial facilities, critical manufacturing, dams, energy, defense industrial base, emergency services, financial, food and agriculture, healthcare and public health, nuclear (reactors, materials and waste), transportation, water and waste water systems, information technology, and government facilities--and have demonstrated intent and capability to disrupt them in case of an international conflict or crisis. The nation lacks a comprehensive and executable strategy to effectively respond [2] Several major factors contribute the nation's unpreparedness. For one, the nation is critically short of cyber security professionals to meet the demand for national cyber defense. For another, Federal government agencies and US policy/laws inadequately prepare, coordinate, share and integrate public and private capabilities to defend the U.S. from a massive cyber disruption. There are more…

Focusing on the first issue, the Department of Defense has identified a critical shortage of cyber security professionals in a number of reports, including, GAO [1] and RAND [2]. The Reserve component was identified as a potential and immediate possibility to lessen the shortage of cyber security/defense professionals. The US Army Reserve (USAR) stands at the threshold of providing significant and critical need to the Federal government, DoD, public and private sector through its new P3i program. This program is designed to understand, identify and fill a strategic opportunity for the USAR to provide an expandable and tailored solution for bridging the civilian and military, cyber security talent gap. Development of a successful USAR Cyber pipeline requires a comprehensive program that starts with our academic partners to build cyber security educational opportunities, as well as develop civilian cyber employment opportunities to maintain skills, maintain relevance and recruit/retain the force and finally a shaping force that contributes to developing a generating force. Toward this end, it is recommended that the DOE Hazardous Materials Management and Emergency Response (HAMMER) Federal Training Center be utilized as the initial cyber security training facility due to its capabilities to bring together Federal, military, and civilian personnel.

CONCLUSIONS / RECOMMENDATIONS

1) The US has an urgent need for an increased number of cyber security experts to protect the US cyberspace from nefarious attacks from foreign nations, terrorist groups, and private hackers.

2) The US needs more centers of academic excellence (CAEs) for providing advanced cyber security education and training to fill the current short fall in the government, military, and private sectors.[1]

3) The DOE HAMMER Federal Training Center is **recommended** to be the initial advanced cyber security training facility. The training program will be under the direction of, and shall be a partnership of, public and private cyber security experts.

4) As the program develops, it is expected to be a model for other centers of excellence for advanced cyber security to be established at other locations to be determined.

BACKGROUND

The threats from cyberspace to our nation are significant. The Director of the National Intelligence, James Clapper, in recent Congressional testimony on the 2013 National Intelligence Estimate (NIE) stated his concern for the defense of the nation from cyber threats. "When it comes to the distinct threat areas, our statement this year leads with cyber and it's hard to overemphasize its significance." [3] The NIE report goes on to warn that we should prepare for increasingly destructive attacks that are designed to render systems inoperable, or could delete critical information, as advanced malware and techniques continue to evolve and proliferate, citing the following 2013 examples:

- In March 2013, South Korea suffered a sizable cyber attack against its commercial and **media** networks, damaging tens of thousands of computer workstations. The attack also disrupted online banking and automated teller machine services [4].

---

[1] 200+ DHS/NSA Centers of Academic Excellence exist across the United States at various colleges and universities, mostly concentrated around the Beltway, the East Coast seaboard through Texas. While these have been engines of dissemination for emerging government standards for cybersecurity education and workforce development (NIST/NICE initiative), there are thousands of universities and colleges that are not aboard and are graduating students with an unawareness of cybersecurity.

- Although likely unrelated to the 2012 network attack against Saudi Aramco, these attacks illustrate an alarming trend in mass data-deletion and system-damaging attacks [5].

Cyber threats could be anything that leads to interruption, meddling or destruction of any valuable service, function or item existing in critical information systems/networks [6]. Whether of "human" or "nonhuman" origin, the threat analysis must scrutinize each element that may bring about conceivable security risk [7]. Cyber threats take many forms from denial-of-service attacks, to beckoning malware, and root access. Today, the actions of nation states, non-state actors, criminal networks, hackivists and terrorist networks are so concerning that the Director of the National Security Agency (NSA) worries that cyber attacks could shut down U.S. critical infrastructure [8]. This could occur for a number of different reasons. For one, nation states see cyberspace capabilities as an asymmetric capability that can level the playing field with a superior economic, diplomatic and military foe like the United States. As early as 1999, Chinese military strategists were envisioning a weaponization of cyberspace as a deterrent to the United States' massive military superiority.

The new trend to create efficiencies and manage economies of scale for the nation's critical infrastructure by leveraging online capabilities is a potential Achilles heel and creates a significant vulnerability. The cyber-physical systems that manage critical infrastructures, called Industrial Control Systems (ICS) and Supervisory Control and Data Acquisition systems (SCADA), run most of the nation's critical infrastructure.

One potential solution to lessen this looming national crisis is to focus the US military's Reserve Component (RC) on the cyber defense mission for the homeland. The Department of Defense can integrate the RC cyber forces to significantly contribute to the defense of national critical infrastructure, provide a partial solution to the massive shortage of cyber security professionals and bridge the information divide between the military, intelligence community, government agencies at the Federal, state and local levels and private industry. Industry is unprepared for seeing itself as a military target. The enemy is too well aware that the United States could be crippled with attacks on the private sector, which owns most of critical infrastructure such as the electric grid and water systems.

Development of a successful USAR Cyber pipeline requires a comprehensive program that starts with our academic partners to build cyber security educational opportunities. This combined with civilian cyber employment opportunities to maintain skills, maintain relevance and recruit/retain the force will lead to shaping a force that contributes to developing a generating force. In order to achieve this goal, an initial training facility must be established. Unfortunately, the current DoD and Army school systems do not yet provide the throughput or advanced skills required for the RC. Thus, it is recommended that the DOE HAMMER Federal Training Center in Richland, Washington be utilized as the initial cyber security training facility due to its capabilities to bring together Federal, military, and civilian personnel in a myriad of programs. HAMMER collaborates with the Pacific Northwest National Laboratory (PNNL) and Washington State University which has a branch campus in Richland. We are suggesting that the collaboration be enlarged to include the University of Washington, an NSA/DHS CAE in cybersecurity education and research and the community college system that is emerging as a network of 2Yr-CAE's.

DISCUSSION

Two senior Chinese People Liberation Army Air Force Colonels published "Unrestricted Warfare" describing a new style of economic, psychological, media and cyber warfare against superior adversary forces, economies and populations [9]. Some reports place the PLA investment in cyberspace operations at 130,000 personnel, more than eighteen times greater than the combined US militaries cyber mission force [10]. Russia has already significantly demonstrated its military cyber power in the conflicts in Estonia, Georgia and Ukraine. In cooperation with the Russian Business Network, the Russian government has generated significant damage to US companies and possesses an advanced, and very sophisticated, cyber attack / exploitation capability. The militarization of cyberspace as a war fighting domain is done. The problem for the United States is that entry into the cyberspace arms race is a low cost, easy and an effective leveler for much smaller, or economically inferior, determined adversaries. The emergence of capabilities such as STUXNET that can effectively destroy physical infrastructure/systems through advanced malware is a disturbing trend for the nation's critical infrastructure. Countries like Syria, Iran, North Korea and terrorist organizations have already proven their cyberattack ability by disrupting US national security targets, businesses and our allies/interests abroad.

Cyberspace enables the United States to run the country and connect multiple infrastructures into a functioning system of systems. This trend will continue as cyberspace expands to the 'internet of things" and integrates cyber-physical systems. These systems, ICS and SCADA, now run most of the nation's critical infrastructure. Unfortunately, we have created serious attack vectors that require only minimal investment and virtual presence to exercise. The homeland is now no longer immune, protected by two oceans and cooperative countries on all sides. We have opened the homeland to ill-intended adversaries that see our country as the enemy. We have given them the tools to penetrate to our core capabilities.

To elaborate, as computers matured over the last 50 years, ICS/SCADA systems have become more networked and integrated into the controls of almost all of the nation's critical infrastructures. For example, ICS systems control execution of concurrent instructions to process controls in refineries, programmed logic controls on the manufacturing floor or Master Terminal Unit (MTU)/Remote Terminal Unit (RTU) in widely distributed SCADA systems that control essential systems such as pipelines, electrical grids and sewage systems [11]. These systems include monolithic (and some of the oldest) standalone, distributed, and networked systems and is about to control the emerging internet of things that will run everything from our households to our cars [12]. Adding to the challenge, these systems of hardware, software, firmware and physical controls blend all generations of systems, making mitigating risks challenging [13]. This is why STUXNET, the advanced malware that attacked the Iranian nuclear centrifuges, is so disturbing to critical infrastructure managers, because many of the vulnerabilities in these systems are not known. They were never designed to withstand attacks in an interconnected world. The engineering emphasis was on safety, not security: two different, although overlapping in some cases, sets of requirements. Additionally, the balance in the private sector between the cost of security versus the bottom line can be challenging. Using the US Army as an example, it has thousands of these systems running everything from garrison sewage, pipelines, power grids, and security systems to weapons system production lines. Those developing and managing these systems have limited knowledge of an ICS/SCADA asset inventory, let alone which systems are networked, connected to the Internet and therefore vulnerable to cyberattack. Critical infrastructure is also effected by policy decisions that impact the maintenance, upkeep, funding and security considerations for much of our publically or government (local, state, federal) controlled ICS/SCADA. The list goes on. We are going through a massive paradigm shift with the information age driving inexorably forward. As a society, this has tested our collective imaginations to understand the unintended consequences like these just described. It makes us vulnerable and hands opportunity to adversaries.

Why is it so hard to defend the nation's critical infrastructure from cyber attack? The management of critical infrastructure has significantly changed over the last 30 years from two thirds publically owned and operated to now two thirds privately owned [14]. This provides some significant challenges in comprehensive cyber security and critical infrastructure protection including legal constraints (the public and private sectors are walled off by legal and regulatory boundaries making cross-sector collaboration on something like a cyberattack challenging), privacy concerns (what are local governments going to do with massive amounts of personal data they collect for everything from taxes to utility bills. Do they understand the privacy and security implications and responsibilities), limited budgets and shortage of personnel (The private sector is prone to see defending against nation state attacks as a Federal government responsibility. Further, they are wedged between profit/loss concerns and rate-payers allergies to increased utility rates).

One major problem for the private sector, like it is for the public sector, is the shortage of qualified and experienced cyber security professionals and their salaries. Both RAND and the Government Accounting Office (GAO) have identified the lack of cyber security professionals in the government and private sector as critical vulnerabilities that need shoring up to achieve the nation's cyber defense [15]. Recent reports have identified shortages of thirty to forty thousand cyber security professionals in the Federal government alone [16]. Further exacerbating the problem, while the government and private sectors have both identified cyber security as a significant threat, they remain far apart on how to act, who acts and when to act. Policy, law and funding inaction from the President and Congress on down have retarded a comprehensive cyber strategy and hurt the Federal government's credibility when it comes to directing cyber defense. (A much need Cyber Security bill has been stalled in Congress for over a year.) Finally, cyberattack information sharing between the public and private sectors has improved but remains critically inadequate in proactively providing assistance for companies under assault.

The US military's Reserve Component (RC) can be a major contributor to the Services and Joint Forces as cyber operators and defenders in the near future. However, successful long term RC cyber support to the Joint Force requires 1) development of an RC Cyber Soldier pipeline for recruiting new/current RC soldiers and transition for the AC (active component) Soldiers, 2) training/education, employment in the cybersecurity profession, and 3) education-training with research infrastructure (TRAIN AS YOU FIGHT). To address this need, the DoD RC Cyber Private Public Partnership was initiated in support of the Chief of the Army Reserve's Private-Public Partnership program (P3). The program is designed to emphasize the professional development, recruiting and retention of cybersecurity talent in the RC. The Cyber P3 lines of effort (LOEs) are nested within USCYBERCOM Commander's strategic vision.

The US relies on information systems and data at every level of national power. US critical infrastructure and military operations are specifically at risk from Advanced Persistent Threats (nation-states, non- state actors, terrorists and criminal networks). The nature of cyber defense has shifted from passive defense (reliance on defense-in-depth and firewalls) to active defense, with an emphasis on highly skilled and critical thinking cyber professionals. It's no longer a matter of if the adversary gets inside our defenses, but when. The probability is 1 [17]. The demand for these individuals far outpaces the Cyber Soldier and unit inventory. The current DoD and Service school systems do not yet provide the throughput or cybersecurity advanced skills required for the RC.

Given that the RC does not have the resources currently, then civilian opportunities (universities and colleges) are the more likely choice for developing and maintaining cyber skills, maintaining continuous skill relevance, recruiting/retaining the right cyberforce, and ultimately a shaping force that contributes to developing a generating force. In order to achieve the latter, an initial training facility must be established very soon. The DoD and Services lack a Cyber Critical Infrastructure advanced training center to develop ICS/SCADA and CI-KR related cyber skills (individual and team-focused). Thus, it is recommended that the DOE HAMMER Federal Training Center in Richland, Washington be utilized as the initial cyber security training facility due to its capabilities to bring together Federal, military, and civilian personnel in a myriad of programs. HAMMER collaborates with the Pacific Northwest National Laboratory (PNNL) and currently conducts military and International Border Security Training (IBST). PNNL, operated by Battelle Memorial Institute's Environmental Molecular Sciences Laboratory (EMSL) is a national scientific user facility located at the PNNL campus in Richland, Washington. EMSL provides experimental and computational resources to address environmental molecular science challenges which have been accelerated when combined with leading-edge hardware, efficient parallel software, accurate and predictive theories and visualization capabilities.

PROGRAM PURPOSE

Current plans underway address organization, training and education and integration with the Army Reserve Component (Army National Guard and US Army Reserve) into the national defense strategy for cyber defense of critical infrastructure. DoD has organized the military cyber force into three strategic echelons with approximately 6000 military cyber personnel and 141 cyber teams [17]. These echelons are the National Mission Force focused on cyber operations outside the US, the Component Commander Support Force focused on support to the six Geographic Combatant Commanders, and the Service support teams focused on providing direct cyber defense support to their Services' (Army, Air Force, Navy, Marines) strategic information systems. None of these forces is focused on employing capabilities beyond the responsibilities of the DoD. The Department of Homeland Security (DHS) is the Federal government's lead agency for defense of critical infrastructure (CI), but they realize that a whole of government approach will be required to proactively respond to CI cyber defense. One way to shore up DHS capabilities is integrating the Army's Reserve Components into DHS and the states' emerging CI cyber defense strategy. Another is to jointly include DOE where their cyber-experience can help both DoD and DHS. Currently, the ARNG and USAR have been directed to stand up twenty-one 39-Soldier Cyber Protection teams (CPT). The CPT has five 7-Soldier sub-teams that are trained to perform missions such as cyber training, policy reviews, penetration testing, counter intrusion, forensics, and vulnerability assessment. These teams are designed to be directly linked to the national intelligence community for integrating real time cyber threat intelligence into the team's operations. The CPTs conduct both routine and crisis response operations to support Cyber Defense Service Providers (CND-SP). The CND-SP in critical infrastructure is similar to the network defense teams supporting ICS/SCADA systems. None of these RC CPTs have been applied to a mission by Army Cyber Command or US Cyber Command. The RC could be integrated in the critical infrastructure cyber defense system through mission requests by DHS, via the 10 FEMA regions, to the DoD. Under similar circumstances, DOE has eight National Laboratories which have excellent experience with computer programs and cyber communications. DOE, together with DoD and DHS, may finally have the knowledge and support to approach a national defense strategy to combat the cyber problems we face as a nation.

Nevertheless, for a successful program it is critical to integrate these RC CPTs prior to crisis so they can identify and understand key cyber terrain (essential hardware, software and cyber-physical systems), train to mission requirements, but more importantly, build relationships with supported public or private critical infrastructure providers. This could be done through deliberate vulnerability assessments partnered with the CI provider or through realistic exercises. Training and education is critical to the CPT success at the individual and team level. The power of the RC is in having civilian-acquired skills linked with military skills that serve dual use in reservists' civilian and military professions. An analog is reserve component doctors and nurses who quickly integrate their extensive medical practice knowledge, skills and attributes when needed by the Army. Another opportunity to demonstrate the value of reservist cyber defense skills is building Cyber public-private partnerships. Army cyber training programs are emerging, but even at maturity would require civilian and academia's assistance to maintain continuous improvement in the CPT soldiers' skills, knowledge, experience and expertise, especially the unique skills needed to defend ICS/SCADA systems.

The development of a public-private partnership would serve all parties by enhancing skills of reserve military personnel, providing a pool of military and university trained and educated cyber professionals available for civilian employment and who provide a catalyst for holistic cyber defense support to the nation's critical infrastructure. In essence, building a cyber defender stool with three supporting legs: the military trained and skilled reserve career directly linked to fulltime civilian cyber professions, aided by continuous education opportunities provided by universities. Additionally, cyber defense training infrastructure is critical to exercise and validate skills, and generate experience and critical multi-agency relationships. Cyber defense in particular is a profession learned by doing, similar to learning a language. Cyber defense critical thinking skills are best developed and tested through immersion in realistic cyber exercise and scenarios. The military motto "train as you fight" fits for cyber defenders. In theory, much of the critical infrastructure exists today in a simulation form with some modifications. This is why we propose, as a potentially viable solution in Washington State, the 88-acre HAMMER facility and its physical training infrastructure. This Federal training facility has numerous critical infrastructure systems replicated and provides a natural location for establishing a closed cyber ICS/SCADA range. In partnership with State's university structure (Washington State University, the University of Washington) and DOE, DHS, Federal intelligence agencies, the State of Washington, US Army Reserves, the WA National Guard, and other industry partners, HAMMER could provide the physical link missing from experimental ranges to help identify, replicate, research, understand and defend against cyber threats to critical infrastructure. The universities could serve as the virtual research cyber range backbone supported by public and private partners.

Missing in Washington State is the physical infrastructure to demonstrate and train against the effects of a cyber attack against cyber-physical systems in a collaborative environment where all partners can research, test, train and work toward cyber resilient networks, systems and people. This concept could fill the void and provide platforms for multiple partners from military, DHS, DOE, law enforcement, state, local and private industry partners to train and exercise together. Additionally, the training partnership could provide a solution to another identified problem which is information sharing. The Federal government generally has access to most of the critical threat information that describes threat intent, capabilities, access points and vectors employed by our cyber adversaries. The reserve CPTs, with additional reserve intelligence capabilities, could serve as a natural link between the intelligence community and state emergency operations or cyber defense centers. Across the country, state threat fusion centers that integrate emergency managers, policy makers, law enforcement, Federal representatives (DHS/FBI) and the military provide opportunities to strengthen information sharing up and down the system about cyber threat and events in real time. Finally, the RC also provides an operational bench of cyber warriors and RC cyber units to retain the Army's expensive investment in ready-trained AC cyber warriors as they transition from active duty. These AC cyber soldiers can also serve as capable civilian employees. With future demand for these RC cyber soldiers and units far outpaces the current inventory, we are providing a national service by creating and nurturing this talent pool of prepared cyber warriors.

Cyber threats to ICS/SCADA and emerging SMART GRID capabilities are a direct threat to national security and the economic well-being of the United States and its allies/partners. The SCADA problem transcends all government agencies (Federal/state/local and tribal), academia and industry. Military reserve components can contribute significantly to the defense of national critical infrastructure, provide a partial solution to the massive shortage of cyber security professionals and bridge the information divide between the military, intelligence community, government agencies at the Federal, state and local levels, and private industry. The HAMMER model provides a useful concept for further strengthening multiple agency response to cyber defense of CI. The ARNG and USAR stands at the threshold of providing significant and critical support to the Federal government, DoD, and the public and private sectors. Cyberspace has become weaponized and the Army must be prepared to operate, defend and maneuver in Cyberspace. The Army should expand, mission, and integrate the ARNG and USAR twenty one CPTs and existing operational cyber capabilities to serve as an immediate surge capability to support national cyber protection of CI.

PROGRAM OBJECTIVES

The Cyber Private Public Partnership is intended to provide a catalyst for building cyber security professionals in the USAR. The Cyber P3 initiative targets: future recruits, initial entry soldiers, transitioning AC soldiers to RC, prior service entering the RC, existing RC soldiers in cyber-related fields and existing professional, cyber-soldiers. The program directly supports the recruiting, retention, transition and cyber skill progression of RC Cyber soldiers across the RC (Support, Training, Operational and Functional Commands). Finally, the program is designed to provide a pool (individuals, units and leaders) of exceptionally qualified and experienced cyber soldiers that can support service, joint and interagency cyber events and operations. The aim is to bridge the civilian-military divide with mutually supporting careers and professional opportunities in cyber security. The program is designed for 3500 - 5000 Army Reserve soldiers and an equal number in the other Service Reserve Components and National Guard.

Cyber security response is best when it is active and proactive versus passive and reactive. The US relies on information systems and data for almost every level of national power. US critical infrastructure and military operations are specifically at risk from Advanced Persistent Threats (nation-states, non- state actors, terrorists and criminal networks). The nature of cyber defense has shifted from passive defense, reliant on defense in depth and firewalls, to active defense, with an emphasis on highly skilled cyber professionals who are critical thinkers. The Reserve Component (RC) in a number of reports including GAO [18] and RAND [19] was identified as a potential and immediate possibility to lessen the shortage of cyber security/defense professionals.

The general threats to our national critical infrastructure can become a system forming factor to help define a model using the U.S. military's reserve component cyber forces to prepare, plan, coordinate, respond, mitigate and recover from a significant cyber attack on the US.

TABLE OF STATE BY STATE CYBERSECURITY CAPABILITIES

State	State involvement / Legal field	CAEs	Cyber security degree programs	CS research centers / facilities	Industry	Grants	Overall
AL	Standard. Main cybersecurity page for the state: http://www.cybersecurity.alabama.gov/ State Information Security Policy: http://cybersecurity.alabama.gov/documents/Policy_600_Information_Security.pdf	Seven NSA/DHS-designated Centers of Academic Excellence	Nine universities offer various degrees	Five research centers at universities	A number of government contractors. Companies: Northrop Grumman, Quantum Research, Boeing, Booz Allen Hamilton, Radiance Technologies	Three CAEs have received SFS grants	Good
AK	Standard/Needs improvement. Alaska's DoA Security website, with links: http://doa.alaska.gov/ets/security/ The State of Alaska was fined $1.7 million for a security breach in 2012: http://www.securitymagazine.com/articles/83272-state-of-alaska-fined--1-7-million-for-security-breach-	One	One university and one college	One	Siemens General Dynamics – IT, AT&T	None found	Low
AZ	Law/policy-wise we couldn't find much. There does not appear to be any state-level cybersecurity policy websites for Arizona.	Three	Three universities offer various degrees	Three	Arizona is growing a "Cybersecurity Valley" with a number of private security companies as well as government contractors who are researching cyber security: Honeywell, Mitre Corporation, Raytheon, General Dynamics C4 Systems, Booz Allen Hamilton, etc.	Two CAEs have received SFS grants. Other NSF grants have also been awarded to University of Arizona, including the AZSecurity Cybersecurity Fellowship program.	Rather good, though can be even better.

State	State involvement / Legal field	CAEs	Cyber security degree programs	CS research centers / facilities	Industry	Grants	Overall
AR	The AR state government seems to promote cybersecurity transparency and education online more than some others. The state government promotes cybersecurity awareness through their sites and observing events such as "National Preparedness Month." Arkansas State Department of Information Systems (DIS) Cyber Security site: http://www.dis.arkansas.gov/security/Pages/default.aspx Arkansas Department of Education Cyber Safety Resources site: http://www.arkansased.org/divisions/learning-services/technology-initiatives-and-resources/cyber-safety-resources	Two	Two universities and one college	Two	Not very many security companies here: AT&T, General Dynamics – IT, etc.	None found	Underdeveloped, though the state government makes an effort.
CA	California envisions their state as a leader in cybersecurity innovation. The state has a robust legislative framework related to information security with some of the earliest data breach laws on the books. The state government engages in cyber awareness exercises and has a cross-sector cybersecurity working group focused on improving the state's posture against security threats and vulnerabilities.	Eight	California has an enormous academic infrastructure with well over a dozen programs tailored towards cybersecurity education in a number of narrowed specialties.	Home to multiple cybersecurity focused research and development centers.	Home not only to the major Silicon Valley companies but also hundreds of small start-ups, niche market companies, and boutique firms providing cybersecurity services.	University funding coming from NSF, DoD, DoE, and other. Grants from cash flushed tech companies / silicon valley firms.	Very good

State	State involvement / Legal field	CAEs	Cyber security degree programs	CS research centers / facilities	Industry	Grants	Overall
CO	Colorado Office of Information Security (OIS) http://www.colorado.gov/cs/Satellite/OIT-Cyber/CBON/1249667675596 The Colorado Office of Information Security is a unit within the Governor's Office of Information Technology and is the single state source for cyber security readiness and awareness. OIS is directly aligned with the goals and objectives of the National Strategy to Secure Cyberspace. Working closely with federal, state, local and private sector partners, the Office of Information Security actively gathers and analyzes information on cyber threats and vulnerabilities that present risk to the state's information systems or the critical information managed within. State Information Security Policies http://www.colorado.gov/cs/Satellite/OIT-Cyber/CBON/1251575408771	Five	Offers a number of offline/online degree programs with focus in cybersecurity through six universities.	Four major centers	A large number of contractors and military presence focusing on cyber security in Colorado, including the Air Force Academy and their associated cyber research center. Colorado Springs was named one of the "Top 5 Cities for Cyber Security Jobs" by clearancejobs.com. Companies include: Northrop Grumman, Lockheed Martin, CenturyLink, Booz Allen Hamilton, Raytheon, etc.	1.25 Million AFOSR equipment grant given to UC Colorado Springs for the Cyber Research Facility	Good
CT	The first state to present a unified cyber security utilities response plan with the Public Utilities Regulatory Authority (PURA). They are working to integrate their activities with DHS. The state has a Cyber security resource page Welcome to CT.Gov/Cybersafe and passed a cyber-bullying law in 2013.	One	7 universities & 3 colleges	Two	UCONN Tech Park $162.3 million investment. state-of-the-art facility for advancing the competitiveness of Connecticut industry, and for the economic success of the state: Comcast, Pratt & Whitney, Hartman International, etc.	A cybersecurity research program underwritten by Comcast (Millions of $$ over three years). DoD - $75 million? $2 million in Fed grants (2012) NCAEIAR	Rather good, though can be even better.

State	State involvement / Legal field	CAEs	Cyber security degree programs	CS research centers / facilities	Industry	Grants	Overall
DC	Evidence shows that the DC metro area is being "remade into the federal government's hub for cybersecurity work." Statistics show DC as having the most cybersecurity job listings in the country.	Five	Virtually all of the academic institutions in DC (at least, five) now offer cybersecurity-related curricula.	Four	DC is fast becoming a hot bed of cybersecurity jobs, most notably, of course, is the federal government and the military; Northrop Grumman, Booz Allen Hamilton, General Dynamics – IT, etc.	One CAE has an SFS scholarship	Good
DE	Delaware is extremely proactive in how it manages and cultivates cybersecurity. There are multiple broad collaborative efforts in progress that will increase the state's ability to secure not only its own assets but to provide talented young cybersecurity professionals to the federal government. Delaware is also one of a number of states to leverage the capabilities of the state's National Guard for cybersecurity.	One	Two universities & two colleges	Delaware lacks the research facility footprint found in many larger states.	The state's cyber efforts are heavily oriented towards intellectual property protection and focused on corporate cyber security: JP Morgan Chase, DuPont, Northrup Grumman, PricewaterhouseCoopers	Regional Cybersecurity Initiative funded by half million dollar NSF grant	Can be much better
FL	Florida recently repealed its security breach law and passed "sweeping legislation" seen as possibly the broadest in the country. The state marked $5 million of their 2015 budget to fund a new state-wide Center for Cyber security. Aim is for Florida to develop cybersecurity as a central pillar of its economic future.	Seven	At least, 15 colleges/universities offering cybersecurity and/or information assurance-focused curricula.	Four	Most of the cyber jobs in FL seem to be with government contractors: BAE, Lockheed Martin, Northrop Grumman, etc.	Four NSF grants	Good

State	State involvement / Legal field	CAEs	Cyber security degree programs	CS research centers / facilities	Industry	Grants	Overall
GA	The state government does not appear to have an office/agency dedicated to security, nor is there a public website providing information on cybersecurity.	Five	Six universities granting cyber security degrees.	Five	Companies: Damballa Labs, Gyrus, Purewire, Dell, Siemens, PwC, Lockheed Martin, Apple, etc.	$10 million DHS project investigating open source, being led by Georgia Tech. One CAE has an SFS scholarship	Rather good, though can be better.
HI	The Hawaiian governor recently appointed a Chief adviser for Technology and Cybersecurity in a move to tighten ties with the federal government and build Hawaii's cybersecurity profile. Recent legislature and state government organizations focus on cyber-crime, cyber bullying/stalking and exploitation of children.	One	Two universities & one college	Four	Booz Allen	The University of Hawaii – West O'ahu received a $245,000 grant from the Office of Naval Research to establish a STEM Center of Excellence at the University.	Can be better
ID	Idaho state government has a cybersecurity awareness website that provides useful links and information for home users, teens, kids, businesses, and educators.	Two	Two universities	Two	Companies: McAfee, CenturyLink, etc.	Two CAEs have SFS scholarships	Can be better

State	State involvement / Legal field	CAEs	Cyber security degree programs	CS research centers / facilities	Industry	Grants	Overall
IL	The governor's office is taking a proactive approach to linking state policy with the development of cyber awareness and building awareness of cybersecurity career fields through well-spaced public relations announcements, attracting veterans into the career field and free on-line competitions through cyber aces and Illinois' CAE2Y. The state proudly displays their involvement in the MSIAS.	Eight	Seven universities & one college	Argonne National Labs: Argonne maintains four laboratory sites - Lemont, Carbondale, Chicago and Champaign.	Companies: BAE Systems Applied Intelligence, Boeing, Booz Allen Hamilton, Deloitte, IBM, KPMG, Lockheed Martin, Northrop Grumman, PwC, Verizon, etc.	In 2010 Illinois received a $1million grant to develop cybersecurity first responded training to be rolled out nationally.	Very good
IN	Indiana has well defined cybersecurity laws and policy. The Universities drive cyber activities within the state, as does the government sector.	Three	Two universities and one college	Four	Companies: Boeing, IBM, PwC, etc.	No data	Can be better
IA	The state has a slow posture regarding cybersecurity laws and government activity. Iowa became only the 43rd state to enact data breach notifications laws.	One	Three universities & one college	Two	Research parks at universities have: BASF, Siemens, etc.	One SFS grant	Can be better

State	State involvement / Legal field	CAEs	Cyber security degree programs	CS research centers / facilities	Industry	Grants	Overall
KS	The state legislation (Chapter 50, Article 7a) specifically addresses issue of Information Security (Cybersecurity) which includes protection of consumer information.	Four	Three universities & one college	One	Companies: HP, etc.	One SFS grant	Can be better
KY	Kentucky is a latecomer to the field in cybersecurity. In 2012, the state finance cabinet posted social security numbers on their website. Recently Kentucky passed two bills which now require local government agencies notify people within 35 days of PII being mishandled or stolen. Kentucky is only the 47th state in the union to pass cybersecurity laws.	Kentucky is one of 7 states without a CAE institution.	Two universities	Nothing found	A bright spot in Kentucky is the job market, possibly because the businesses are trying to come up to speed with the rest of the pack. Companies: Time Warner Cable, Kforce, etc.	Nothing found	Low
LA	Legislation Act 772 – 2001 regulates all Information Technology related policies. This includes IT Governance, Security Policies, Computer Infrastructure and General Policies. This has been revised with few additions (La. Rev. Stat. § 51:3071 et seq. (Acts 2005, No. 499, §1, eff. Jan. 1, 2006.))	Three	Three universities & one college	Four	Companies: IBM, etc.	Nothing found	Can be better

State	State involvement / Legal field	CAEs	Cyber security degree programs	CS research centers / facilities	Industry	Grants	Overall
ME	Maine does not have a generally high level of cybersecurity activity, but the state has the requisite data breach laws and a relatively active state government offering information and participating in some conferences targeting IA/CD. The research and education capacity of the state is rather small.	None yet, but the NSA and DHS are designating the seven-school system a National CAE in IA and Cyber security: http://www.pressherald.com/2014/11/21/maine-universities-recognized-for-cybersecurity-education/	Two universities	Two	There is about 900 job offers in information security field in Maine according to Indeed: http://www.indeed.com/q-Information-Security-l-Maine-jobs.html	$1 million in grants from the National Science Foundation and Maine Technology Institute to design and build cyber security lab at USM.	Needs serious improvement, and there are good efforts to achieve that.
MD	Tons of state backing. Examples: Implementation of a cyber investment tax credit for companies as an incentive. Creation of a Commission on Cybersecurity Innovation and Excellence. Creation of a Resource Center for Cybersecurity (co-led by Maryland and Michigan). Creation of a Baltimore / Washington task force to implement a strategy for cyber around CYBERCOM activities. Creation of a Director of Cyber Development.	16	16 universities, colleges or tech institutes that offer degrees or certificates in cyber.	Six. Also, nearby federal agencies and institutions offer a significant strategic advantage. For example, they are located by: NIST, CYBERCOM, NSA/CSS, NASA High Performance Computing Center-2; schedule for completion in 2016 to be located at Ft. Meade.	Venture Capital Deals: 374 from 2008-2012 in cybersecurity valued at $2,096,999,000. There are over 75,000 employed in Cyber Security-related jobs in the Greater Baltimore/Central Maryland region. In addition, there are nearly 20,000 open Cyber Security job positions in Maryland. There are currently more than 11,000 companies in Maryland that create products and services to protect against cyber-attacks, including heavy hitters such as Northrop Grumman, JHU APL, Verizon, Lockheed, Booz Allen, SAIC, and CSC.	TEDCO fund invests in start-up cyber security technologies for Maryland based companies with more than 16 full-time employees and less than $500,000 in outside investments. Investments per company will not exceed $100,000.	Excellent

State	State involvement / Legal field	CAEs	Cyber security degree programs	CS research centers / facilities	Industry	Grants	Overall
MA	Should likely be considered as one of the model states regarding IA/CD capability. The state has standard cybersecurity, cyberbullying, and identity theft laws and a fairly active state government that recognizes and supports the advancement of cybersecurity as a strategic need. The state is one of six in the US that has developed and utilizes the Cyber Aces (http://www.cyberaces.org/) program. The program is a cybersecurity talent development effort using competitions to select promising students for cybersecurity education and internship opportunities.	Four: Boston University, Northeastern University, Worcester Polytechnic University, and University of Massachusetts – Amherst. Additionally, Massachusetts is home to two of the nation's most prestigious and technically advanced universities: Harvard and MIT.	The following institutions offering varying cybersecurity degree options: Bay Path University, Boston University, Worcester Polytechnic, University of Massachusetts, Northeastern University, Mass Bay Community College, Brandeis, and many affiliate universities in the University of Massachusetts system.	The state is home to two major cybersecurity research organizations with the MITRE Corporation's Bedford location and Lincoln Labs at MIT. There are many other smaller centers, organizations, and working groups operating in both industry and academia.	The state has companies with cybersecurity missions in all the major sectors like finance, defense, tech, government, healthcare, and energy, including: Akamai Facebook, Liberty Mutual Group, Pfizer Inc., etc.	The academic institutions are massively funded through federal grants.	Good
MI	Michigan has a long standing tradition of building and maintaining collaborative internet/security relationships. The legislature passed three cybersecurity laws, Identity Theft Protection Act 452, Social Security Number Privacy Act and the Michigan Anti-spam laws.	Five: Davenport University, Eastern Michigan University, Ferris State University, University of Detroit, Mercy, Walsh College.	Six universities & one college	Three	Sponsors for the Michigan State conference include companies such as AT&T, Deloitt, Comcast, Symantec, Unisys, IBM, Cisco, MicroSoft, Motorola, ITC, Sprint, etc.	The State is pulling together a $3 billion private public initiative, "Pure Michigan Business Connect" to promote entrepreneurship to capital and a 'cyber security business environment'	Good

State	State involvement / Legal field	CAEs	Cyber security degree programs	CS research centers / facilities	Industry	Grants	Overall
MN	The State through the collaboration with the non-profit organization, Advance IT Minnesota, is positioning Minnesota as a top-ten regional economy for information technology careers as measured by total IT-related employment. Through a strong quality education system which has increased enrollment in IT 76% since 2006.	Six: Inver Hills Community College and Minneapolis Community and Technical College are CAE/2Y. Capella University, Metropolitan State University, St Cloud State University and the University of Minnesota are all CAE/IAE.	Four universities & two colleges	Two	Companies: Honeywell, Alliant Tech Systems Inc., etc.	No data	Rather good, though can be even better.
MS	The State's cybersecurity profile and prominence is tied closely with the success and maturity of Mississippi State University (MSSU). The State has updated its cybercrime, cyber bullying and cyber stalking laws. The website is clearly laid out a policies are up-to-date. The state and MSSU has close ties to the FBI and DHS.	Mississippi State University is the only university ranked as a CAE in Mississippi; but the school holds all three designations, CAE, CAE-R and IA. The University has a strong reputation for digital forensics and working with veterans, collaborating with the FBI, DHS and other three letter agencies.	MSSU is ranked by the Ponemon Institute as the third best university to study cybersecurity in the country.	A fair number of military installations, Columbus and Kessler AFB, Camp Shelby Army Base and the Navy's Gulfport Battalion Center and the Naval Air Station (NAS) Meridian. Stennis Space Center	Companies: Apex Lockheed Martin, Raytheon, etc.	No data	Relatively good

State	State involvement / Legal field	CAEs	Cyber security degree programs	CS research centers / facilities	Industry	Grants	Overall
MO	Missouri's Mission for cybersecurity is to promote and provide expertise in information security management for all state agencies and support national and local homeland information security efforts. Their Vision is to be a leader in preserving the confidentiality, integrity, and availability of state data and dependent resources while maintaining efficient and effective operations. Missouri passed cyber bullying and cyber stalking legislation in 2013.	Missouri has two centers of academic excellence, Missouri University of Science and Technology (CAE/IAE,CAE/R and the University of Missouri- Columbia, a CAE/IAE.	Seven universities	Two	Companies: Boeing, IBM, L3 Communications, Booz Allen Hamilton, Honeywell, MasterCard, etc.	No data	Relatively good
MT	Montana has a standard data breach notification laws (2-6-504. Notification of breach of security of data system & MONT CODE ANN § 30-14-1704: Montana Code - Section 30-14-1704: Computer security breach) that can be found at http://leg.mt.gov/bills/mca/2/6/2-6-504.htm. The state government provides a relatively exhaustive information security webpage (http://infosec.mt.gov/default.mcpx) and the state does have a CISO position as of 2013.	Montana is one of a just a handful of states that do not have any NSA approved centers of excellence.	One university & one college	Montana does not host any major cybersecurity research centers (national labs, FFRDCs, etc.) and the bulk of their research on IA is by academics.	Montana does not have a large specialized cybersecurity industry. There are a number of small boutique security and analytics companies that have taken advantage of Montana's low cost of living.	Using NSF funding University of Montana created a new Cyber Innovation Laboratory dubbed "Cyberlab" that is focused on IA and other relevant tech topics.	Rather low, though can be improving.

State	State involvement / Legal field	CAEs	Cyber security degree programs	CS research centers / facilities	Industry	Grants	Overall
NE	They have fairly strong data breach laws, a proactive state government. Their state government has a good reputation and hosts conferences and is active in outreach and organizing. Nebraska has a fairly standard and robust set of data breach notification laws with their Nebraska Revised Statute 87-801:807 that were first enacted in 2006. The state has a published IS policy updated as of 2013 that can be found at http://nitc.nebraska.gov/standards/8-101.html The state has a specific but limited cybersecurity web presence with http://www.cio.nebraska.gov/cyber-sec/index.html.	There are two NSA approved CAEs at the University of Nebraska at Omaha (UNO) and Bellevue University.	Two universities	Nebraska does not have the national labs or FFRDCs found in other states but their academic community appears to be relatively active and cooperative in cybersecurity studies.	Aside from the ubiquitous military industrial complex companies that work in cybersecurity and a number of smaller information security consultancies there are not many large specialized cybersecurity firms in Nebraska.	No data	Relatively good, but can be better.
NV	The state has some of the more stringent data breach and data security laws on its books. Particularly, Nevada has mandated PCI-DSS for companies operating in the state with payment cards. Nevada also has a CISO position with an Office of Information Security located in their Enterprise IT department. Since 1999 Nevada has had a Technological Crime Advisory Board that focuses to some degree on electronic crimes like identity theft, online fraud, etc.	Nevada has one NSA center of academic excellence with the University of Nevada Las Vegas.	Two universities & one college	Historically, Nevada has been very involved in nuclear testing and nuclear security and some of these agencies have limited cybersecurity R&D mission sets related to protecting the nuclear stockpile and weapon design information.	The enormous gaming industry has considerable interest in cybersecurity but specific information is not particularly easy to come by since the companies are highly competitive. The defense industry also maintains facilities in Nevada providing consulting and R&D services (CACI, Lockheed, etc.).	The historic relevance of nuclear energy and weapon testing means there is some cooperation between the state of Nevada and its companies/agencies and the US Department of Energy.	Can be better.

State	State involvement / Legal field	CAEs	Cyber security degree programs	CS research centers / facilities	Industry	Grants	Overall
NH	New Hampshire has a fairly robust data breach notification law that incorporates many of the elements found in other states throughout the US. NH has a devoted cybersecurity webpage on the state government's Information Technology site offering best practices, guidance, and basic threat alert information. The site can be viewed here: http://www.nh.gov/doit/cybersecurity/	New Hampshire has only Dartmouth College which holds the CAE-Research designation.	Two universities & one college.	There are no national laboratories or Federally Funded Research and Development Centers located in New Hampshire. That said, Dartmouth College developed and currently managed the Institute for Information Infrastructure Protection (I3P).	New Hampshire expects to see "professional, scientific, and technical services . . . [to grow] nearly 24 percent" between the years of 2010 and 2020. -- http://www.cybersecurityu.org/new-hampshire-steady-economy-attracts-cyber-professionals/ Some major information security employers in the state are BAE Systems, Bank of America, the State Government of NH, and Liberty Mutual.	Dartmouth College collects considerable grants (cursory search of awards is well over $2,000,000) from federal funding sources.	Rather good considering its relatively small size.
NJ	Data breach and cyber-bullying laws with a very involved state government and state police force. New Jersey has a number of cyber related government offices and bodies including a state ISAC, a department of information security with a portal, and a state homeland security & preparedness organization with a cyber-mission. The state police also have an information security unit and other IT related groups working on technology crime and researching means by which crime can more effectively be dealt with through leveraging technological assets. They also appear to have Cyber Aces and Cyber Patriot programs running that seek to educate and develop cyber talent.	Six CAEs with a variety of academic research centers contributing to theory and practice	Six universities	New Jersey has one FFRDC with the Princeton Plasma Physics Laboratory, to research cutting edge physics and nuclear fusion. Their cybersecurity relevance is nebulous at best. The major research and practice centers are located at the state's many educational institutions.	New Jersey is slotted as a major growth state for tech jobs and has established clusters in the financial services and bio-tech industries.	No data	Rather good, though can be even better.

State	State involvement / Legal field	CAEs	Cyber security degree programs	CS research centers / facilities	Industry	Grants	Overall
NM	The state is among the last in the US to enact any sort of comprehensive data breach protection law, going without such a statue until early 2014. NM has an ISAC as part of the compulsory national strategy and they have state-level homeland security and emergency management office. The state IT department publishes their security policies which appear fairly standard.	Two	Two universities	Sandia National Laboratory and Los Alamos National Laboratory: SCADA security, analytics, education, insider threat detection, energy grid security, quantum cryptography, malware classification, etc.).	New Mexico has a couple of industrial clusters with some relevance to cybersecurity. The presence of Kirtland AFB and a number of national labs bring in many Aerospace companies like Honeywell and Lockheed. There is some tech involvement (small Intel plant, etc.).	The University of New Mexico's Center for Information Assurance Research and Education has a SFS program.	Rather good, but can be better.
NY	New York is following close behind California in the legislative aspect of cyber regulations. Their focus is on financial and business repercussions of cyber security and the impact to national and international financial systems. In 2013 Governor Cuomo established a Cyber Security Advisory Board to guide state government on developments in cyber security and make recommendations for protecting the state's critical infrastructure and information systems. New York's governor is working to position New York as a leader in cybersecurity to attract the growing industry of cyber-related business to the state. Focus on the banking industry is a major strategy and NYS Department of Financial Services has "'required' 200 banks to assess cyber policies and processes."	Eight	Ten universities & two colleges	Three	There is an extensive list of accounting, consulting and law firms focused on the growing sector of cyber security related business.	No data	Very good

State	State involvement / Legal field	CAEs	Cyber security degree programs	CS research centers / facilities	Industry	Grants	Overall
NC	As of October 1, 2009, entities doing business in North Carolina will be required to both provide more detailed data breach notices to individuals and be more forthcoming with the state's attorney general. NC DOJ provides best practice information to residents through alerts and news articles on their webpage. North Carolina has created a cyber-information sharing and analysis center that is part of the larger Multi-State ISAC. The NC-ISAC provides a central resource for gathering information on cyber threats to critical infrastructure from state agencies and providing two-way sharing of information between and among the state agencies and with local government where permissible. NC has an office of Enterprise Security & Risk Management that provides state information security policies and procedures, awareness and training services, threat response, and secure IT procurement directives as part of the NC CIO's and CISO's responsibilities. The NC National Guard is being utilized for state cyber exercises	There are four NSA CAEs located in North Carolina at UNC-Charlotte, East Carolina University, NC State University, and North Carolina A&T State University.	Six universities & several colleges	There are research centers working on the majority of key cybersecurity topics with special attention being paid to big data, high performance computing, electric grid security, and embedded systems security.	The Research Triangle Park's security relevant tenants are as follows: IBM, Cisco, NetApp, Red Hat, EMC, GE, Lenovo, Qualcomm, Sony Ericsson, and Verizon and others. There are numerous bio-tech firms as well as a large DuPont chemical facility that likely contribute to some of the state's focus on protecting IP and securing data. NC is also home to Duke Energy which is absolutely one of the largest energy utilities in America and thus there's considerable focus on grid security, next-gen cyber physical systems, and embedded systems security. There is also huge interest and activity in big data and cloud computing. NC State is the alma mater of the founders of the software and analytics giant SAS and they maintain a large presence in the state.	The state's many collaborative research projects that span academia and industry attract fairly enormous funding from the NSF, DOD, and Intelligence Community. NC cyber research projects include a $60 million funding grant from the NSA and more than 20 currently active NSF cybersecurity grant awards that exceed $500,000.	Good

State	State involvement / Legal field	CAEs	Cyber security degree programs	CS research centers / facilities	Industry	Grants	Overall
ND	North Dakota has a fairly standard data breach notification law on their books that was last updated in 2013 to include a person's health insurance information. They also have a cyber-bullying law in place as of 2013. The state government does have an office of IT Security and there is a state CISO. The ND state government's IT Security department maintains a webpage with best practices, alerts, and other guidance but it appears to be only infrequently updated. There exists a ND state government office focusing on homeland security and emergency services but there appears to be limited focus on cyber planning or exercises. The state is part of a Multi-State ISAC through DHS.	None.	One brick and mortar cybersecurity degree program at an institution called Rasmussen College in Fargo/Bismarck, ND. One place offering Forensics specialization at Southwestern Community College.	No evidence of private, public, or pseudo-public institutions or groups engaged in specialized cybersecurity research or practice.	Outside of the ubiquitous presence of Military Industrial Complex companies that do cybersecurity contracting there appears to be little commercial focus on cybersecurity in ND.	No data	Low.

State	State involvement / Legal field	CAEs	Cyber security degree programs	CS research centers / facilities	Industry	Grants	Overall
OH	Ohio has a fairly standard data breach notification law and they do have both a CISO and a Chief Privacy Officer for the state. The state does maintain a centralized privacy and security webpage to inform citizens about cybersecurity issues and to offer best practices guidelines for its residents. Past cybersecurity incidents (Anonymous hacking the state's web portal) seem to be pushing the state forward on cybersecurity.	Four (Air Force Institute of Technology, Ohio State University, Owens Community College and Sinclair Community College).	Ohio has four centers of excellence and a handful of other four year schools providing cybersecurity education. The state also has a large quantity of cybersecurity education being delivered through the two-year community college system. Altogether: eight universities & four colleges.	The state does have a number of large research universities like Ohio State and Cincinnati working on information security.	Companies: Verizon, Booz Allen Hamilton, JP Morgan Chase, Northrup Grumman, GE, IBM, Battelle	The Ohio Third Frontier Commission approved $5 million to support the Columbus Collaboratory, a multiple industry partnership to make Ohio a leader in advanced analytics and cybersecurity. A $20 million investment will come from American Electric Power, Battelle, Cardinal Health, Huntington Bank, L Brands, Nationwide and OhioHealth.	Good

State	State involvement / Legal field	CAEs	Cyber security degree programs	CS research centers / facilities	Industry	Grants	Overall
OK	Oklahoma clearly defined its IT/Cybersecurity policies and procedures in 2003 with updates to their on-line manual in 2011. The state meetings regularly with its agencies and conducts quarterly meetings, table exercises and integrates their activities with the OK Homeland Security Department. The "Oklahoma Computer Crimes Act" initiated 1984 with updates related to cybercrimes, initially crimes involved with computers. http://www.forwardedge2.com/pdf/OK-laws.pdf; penalties ran from $5000 to $100,000 in penalties with jail time. 24 Okla. Stat. § 161 et seq. passed in 2008 lays out guidelines for security breech notification within Oklahoma. The state is running the Oklahoma's Cyber Command.	Oklahoma has six Centers for Academic Excellence and Research. Four are two year schools: Francis Tuttle Technology School, Oklahoma City Community College, Oklahoma Department of Career & Technology and Rose State College. Oklahoma State University and University of Tulsa are the four year CAEs.	Within the 29 technology centers at 58 campus sites, a range of cybersecurity courses, including networking through higher level certification courses at the CAE-R 2Y are available.	Three	Oklahoma has a strong DHS presence, with the major accounting firms, Deloitte, Price Waterhouse; Microsoft, major defense contractors and smaller home grown companies have positions relative to cybersecurity work at Fort Sills and Tinker AFB. The major companies, Microsoft, Google, CISCO and others have a presence in Oklahoma.	Oklahoma's 2004 NSF $3 million grant built a strong 2 year/4 year educational network. In 2007 an additional $2.7 million developed a deeper connection to workforce development.	Good

State	State involvement / Legal field	CAEs	Cyber security degree programs	CS research centers / facilities	Industry	Grants	Overall
OR	Oregon has a standard data breach notification law on their books that was enacted in 2007 (§ 646A.604). Additionally they have the Oregon Identity Theft Protection Act (http://www.cbs.state.or.us/dfcs/id_theft.html) and proposing digital privacy legislation. The state government offers a fairly standard website for enterprise security and information security resources, providing basic guidance, best practices, and news related to information security. Oregon participated in the Department of Homeland Security's CyberStorm IV exercises. Through CS IV, DHS designed, conducted, and evaluated exercises for seven states including: Maine, Oregon, Washington, Idaho, Missouri, Mississippi, and Nevada. Oregon has taken efforts to extend information security learning down to elementary and high school level education. The Education Information Security Council (EISC) is responsible.	The only Center of Academic Excellence in Oregon was located at Portland State University (PSU). The National Security Agency (NSA) designated Portland State University as a Center of Academic Excellence in Information Assurance Education in 2003: http://www.pdx.edu/news/nsa-designates-portland-state-quotcenter-academic-excellence-information-assurance-educationquot But not anymore: https://www.nsa.gov/ia/academic_outreach/nat_cae/institutions.shtml	The educational component is relatively small but there appears to be active engagement and research going on at schools like Portland State, Univ. of Oregon, and Oregon State University as well as a number of options for two-year education.	The state does not have major cybersecurity relevant national labs or FFRDCs but has a number of organizations and institutions engaging in IA research both privately and publically. At University of Oregon there are a couple of ongoing research partnerships and academic centers performing cybersecurity research, publishing, and tool building.	The state has a respectable tech and software industry base making security products, solutions, and hardware. According to an OSU news article "there are about 20 companies in Oregon doing computer security-related work, one of the largest concentrations of cyber-security industry experts in the nation." – http://oregonstate.edu/ua/ncs/archives/2012/aug/oregon-front-lines-fighting-cyber-terrorism Specifically, some of those companies includes Flir Systems, ID Experts, EID Passport, Kryptiq and Tripwire. As well as, Mentor Graphics and Intel – working with its McAfee subsidiary – are developing hardware-based technologies to guard against online snooping. As part of their outreach program on cyber education, Oregon has set up "The Oregon Centre for Cyber Excellence (OCE)". The purpose is to be a national asset to advance substantially the knowledge and educational strategies for cyber-education. They are collaborating with Colleges and Universities in the state.	Source of Funding: Federal support, industry funding and National Security Foundation (NSF), Intel, Google, MIT Lincoln Labs, Battelle and ARO. Total research funding to date is about $8.49 million.	Relatively good.

State	State involvement / Legal field	CAEs	Cyber security degree programs	CS research centers / facilities	Industry	Grants	Overall
PA	PA's Governor has spoken about the importance of public/private partnerships in securing critical infrastructure. Pennsylvania's Information Security Office has a pretty comprehensive website with information for residents about their department, security awareness, and resources. The Pennsylvania Information Sharing and Analysis Center (PA-ISAC) was established to address the Commonwealth of Pennsylvania's cyber security readiness and critical infrastructure coordination. This initiative is led by the Chief Information Security Officer for the Commonwealth of Pennsylvania's Office for Technology, responsible for leading and coordinating the Commonwealth's efforts regarding cyber readiness and resilience. Pennsylvania has a CERT team: PA-CSIRT, the Commonwealth of Pennsylvania's Computer Incident Response Team.	Pennsylvania currently has 7 NSA/DHS-designated academic Centers of Excellence, four of which offer SFS scholarships. Carnegie Mellon University (CMU) is a national leader in cybersecurity research and education and one of the few NSA-designated CAEs in Cyber Operations.	Three out of seven PA schools were ranked in the top 10 for cybersecurity education by the Ponemon Institute (Carnegie Mellon, U of Pittsburgh, West Chester U).	PA has seven of the nation's leading cybersecurity research centers, most notably at CMU.	Companies: The National Cyber-Forensics & Training Alliance, H-Bar Cyber Solutions, Wombat Security, Dell, Software Engineering Institute at Carnegie Mellon University, Lockheed Martin, BAE Systems	NSF Scholarship for Service grants awarded to four universities.	Very good.

State	State involvement / Legal field	CAEs	Cyber security degree programs	CS research centers / facilities	Industry	Grants	Overall
RI	In 2011 the Rhode Island Cyber Disruption Team (RICDT) was established, whose mission is to prevent and respond to cyber security events and defend the security of critical infrastructure. The RICDT is comprised of members from the Rhode Island State Police Computer Crimes Unit and individuals representing higher education, hospitals, finance, utilities and defense. The following year the state released RI Statewide Cyber Strategic Plan. RI is one of a few states—including Massachusetts, California, Connecticut, Oregon, Maryland, and Nevada—have also enacted laws requiring businesses to maintain data security standards to protect state residents' personal information from being compromised.	University of Rhode Island is the only CAE CAER/IAE in the state.	Three universities	Two	Companies: Cybercoders, The Judge Group, Corvus Technology Resources, CVS, Atrion, CVS Caremark, CharterCARE Health Partners, OSHEAN, Corvus, Technology Resources, Carousel Industries, GTECH	Verizon Foundation has awarded a $15,000 grant to the Salve University to further the Pell Center for International Relations and Public Policy's efforts in helping to bolster cybersecurity in Rhode Island companies.	Rather low, can be better.
SC	South Carolina instituted cybersecurity stalking, harassment and anti-bullying laws in 2012-13 legislative sessions. The State has awarded Deloitte contracts for incident response. The initial reports – SC needs to establish and mature its cybersecurity profile across the state government and there will be a need for long-term commitment of funding to bring the state up to an acceptable level of performance. As this report was filed in 2014, legislation is in the process of being developed. The State connects to MSISAC and DHS.	University of South Carolina is the only CAE/IAE - is a new center with a focus on engineering – specifically securing wired and unwired network and security protocol development for networks and distributed systems.	One	One	The Advanced Security Technology Research Alliance (ASTRA).	ASTRA has received a $50,000 grant from the Trident Workforce Investment Board to offer two training programs in the Charleston area.	Low, needs improvement.

State	State involvement / Legal field	CAEs	Cyber security degree programs	CS research centers / facilities	Industry	Grants	Overall
SD	The state is one of three in the US that has failed to set up data breach notification laws and appears to engage very little in state government cybersecurity promotion, awareness, and education. Their cyber security legislation is pending for 2015. There is a very limited cybersecurity web portal provided by the state government that largely offers links to federal resources on information assurance.	Dakota State University is the only CAE/IAE in the state South Dakota and received the designation in 2012-13.	The state has a small education system but is home to a premier cybersecurity school with Dakota State University. Its B.S. in Cyber Operations is being augmented with a new doctoral degree in cybersecurity in Fall 2014. South Dakota State University (SDSU) also offers degree programs in information security.	There are no major research centers or companies but two interesting academic research project.	Secure Banking Solutions (SBS). The need for security professionals is also for companies: SCN Communications, S2Technologies, Stinger Ghaffarian Technologies, Black Hills Corporation.	In 2013 the Legislature appropriated $900,000 to fund Dakota State University's information systems programs and cyber security programs.	Rather low

State	State involvement / Legal field	CAEs	Cyber security degree programs	CS research centers / facilities	Industry	Grants	Overall
TN	Tennessee State Government seems to have a limited presence on cybersecurity. The Governor has proclaimed October Cybersecurity Month and the Department of Finance is taking the 'lead' with a 38 page Policy Manual. Tennessee has enacted Cybersecurity Breach Law.	There are one two-year, Jackson State Community College, and three CAE/IAE universities: Fountainhead College of Technology, University of Memphis, and University of Tennessee at Chattanooga.	Four universities and one college	Oakridge National Laboratory (ORNL)'s Cyber Information Security Research (CISR).	There is extensive corporate presence buzzing around ORNL and the rest of the state. Deloitte, Addeco, Apex Systems, Cadre Information Security, Booz Allen Hamilton, IBM, The Hinkle Group have a presence in the state.	No data	Relatively good
TX	This state is VERY invested in cybersecurity. State cyber laws and policies are outline in the "Texas Cybersecurity Framework" http://www.dir.state.tx.us/security/policy/Pages/framework.aspx	Texas has 16 NSA/DHS-designated Centers of Excellence.	Dozens of colleges/universities . UT San Antonio was ranked as the #1 university for cybersecurity by HP / Ponemon in 2014.	San Antonio has been dubbed "Cyber City USA" due it being the home of the Air Force Cyber Command as well as the National Security Agency's Texas Cryptology Center, a new National Security Agency data center.	Nearly 80 defense contractors, including dozens focused on information security.	Four of the CAEs offer SFS scholarships. Also, NSF grant award of $284,000 to The San Antonio College (SAC) Department of Computer Information Systems (CIS)	Excellent

State	State involvement / Legal field	CAEs	Cyber security degree programs	CS research centers / facilities	Industry	Grants	Overall
UT	"We have a rich history in defense, IT, and in a lot of other business sectors, as well," said Gary Harter, Executive Director of Veteran's Affairs with the Utah Governor's Office of Economic Development." A number of companies tell us they like coming to Utah, and they like hiring in Utah, because they find good success with employees in Utah who can readily get security clearances." The state also offers a number of incentives for business, including low energy and utility costs and reasonable permitting and regulation.	Only has one university that is designated as a CAE.	Four universities.	NSA recently built their massive data center there. Also, Space Dynamics Laboratory – Utah State University.	Salt Lake City was named by ClearanceJobs.com as one of the top 5 cities for cybersecurity companies. There is a notable presence of government and contractors in the area. Companies: Raytheon, FireEye, AccessData, Northrop Grumman	Utah Valley University received a $3 million grant for cybersecurity training from the Department of Labor.	Relatively good.
VT	The governor has integrated services and policies reflecting a well-integrated approach to communicating with multiple audiences through an easy to use state website: www.itsecurity.vermont.gov. IT policies ranging from 2004 to 2012 have been updated to reflect Vermont's review of 'hot topics' such as Mobile Devices. Cyberbullying is covered by State Law 16 and passed a Security Breach Notification Law in 2012.	Vermont has two centers of academic excellence: Champlain College and Norwich University.	One university and one college.	Four	S2Technologies There were 21 open cybersecurity positions through Indeed related to activities at St. Albans AFB in Vermont.	Pwnie Express in 2013 raised $5.1 million to test wireless devices and networks in remote locations.	Relatively low.

State	State involvement / Legal field	CAEs	Cyber security degree programs	CS research centers / facilities	Industry	Grants	Overall
VA	Virginia has two distinct security breach disclosure and notification laws that separately cover both personal information and private healthcare related information. The laws are similar to those found in many US states and provide definitions on the types of data to be secured and the mechanisms by which companies must notify victims of a breach. In 2014, Virginia governor Terry McAuliffe created the Virginia Cybersecurity Commission that has been tasked with identifying high risk security threats, promoting cybersecurity awareness and offering expert input related to the security of state networks and information assets. The Commission includes former US Cybersecurity "Czar" Richard A. Clarke.	The state is home to seven NSA Centers of Academic Excellence and those programs benefit greatly from their relative proximity to the US federal government.	Eight universities and one college.	Virginia is home to a huge number of federal agencies that have cybersecurity responsibilities. DHS has NCCIC and US CERT in Arlington. Additionally, MITRE Corp has long maintained a large facility in Northern Virginia.	General Dynamics, Lockheed Martin, Boeing, Booz Allen	Massive funding…given proximity to DoD, NSF, NASA, etc.	Good

State	State involvement / Legal field	CAEs	Cyber security degree programs	CS research centers / facilities	Industry	Grants	Overall
WA	Washington State enacted an anti-cyber-stalking group early on. The legislature has enacted cyberbullying legislation and there is pending legislation in HB 1365-2013-14 requiring cities and counties to provide higher levels of security for their courts. Washington State is active in the MRSC and has a strong relationship with the Department of Homeland Security (via PRISEM). Association of Washington Cities promotes cyber security across the state.	One university and two colleges.	Six universities and seven colleges.	Pacific Northwest National Labs headquartered in Richland, WA, PNNL maintains offices in Seattle and concentrates cybersecurity research in several areas.	Seattle and the East Side, Bellevue, Kirkland, Redmond support strong cyber security business climates. Washington State is the home of Microsoft, Amazon, Starbucks, Boeing; companies with high cyber security needs. Google has developed a presence and IBM, Booz Hamilton, Deloitte and a myriad of government focused contractors are attracted to JBLM, Fairchild AFB, Bangor Naval Base/Bremerton Shipyard. Additional companies include Verizon Wireless, T-Mobile, etc.	PRISEM, in collaboration with WA State Dept. of Commerce, has received funding to transition to a non-profit business model.	Relatively good, but can be even better.

State	State involvement / Legal field	CAEs	Cyber security degree programs	CS research centers / facilities	Industry	Grants	Overall
WV	West Virginia's Office of Technology Cyber Security Program won an award in 2011 for Risk Management Initiatives. Executive Order 6-06 called for the formation of an Executive Branch Information Security Team and a Privacy Management Team. The Governor's Executive Information Security Team (GEIST) was subsequently established which enlisted high-level departmental operatives to extend the reach of the Office of Information Security and Controls. An Information Security Strategic Plan was developed and, over time, resources and tools have been acquired to focus on the information and cybersecurity challenge of overall risk reduction through strong controls and heightened awareness. In addition, an audit function was established at the Office of Technology.	Two	One university and one college.	Two	Companies: Lockheed Martin, TASC, SecureStrux LLC, FireEye, Mitre Corporation, Criterion Systems	None found.	Relatively low.
WI	The state has a "Ready Wisconsin" site, part of WI's emergency management efforts and in line with DHS's "Ready" campaign, promotes cybersecurity awareness and safety tips and links for citizens. There is also a state Bureau of Security.	None	One university and one college.	Three	Companies: Wisconsin Security Research Consortium, USIS	Researchers at UW-Madison received a portion of a large federal grant for developing secure software for infrastructure systems. Also, Collaborative Research grant from the NSF for Wisconsin Collaborating Campuses on Cyber Security.	Low

State	State involvement / Legal field	CAEs	Cyber security degree programs	CS research centers / facilities	Industry	Grants	Overall
WY	Governor Mead has been pushing for betting Internet access in the state of Wyoming. The governor is aware of cybersecurity issues and the state government website provides helpful links for information/awareness. WY has pretty standard Electronic Crime statues.	None	One college.	One	Companies: Green House Data	None found.	Low.

State	State involvement / Legal field	CAEs	Cyber security degree programs	CS research centers / facilities	Industry	Grants	Overall
PR	According to the IC3 Internet Crime Report for 2013, Puerto Rico ranked ninth globally in terms of total victim complaints related to cybercrime with 550, placing the island above such nations as Brazil, France, Germany, Russia, Italy, China and Japan. A large proportion of these attacks are targeted at banks with the intent to steal sensitive data, including account numbers and other financial information. In Puerto Rico, there are two units dedicated to investigating cybercrimes on the island: the Cybercrimes Division at the Police Department and the Cybercrimes Investigation Unit at the Justice Department. Several attempts were made to establish a definitive public policy on the prosecution of cybercrime through local House Bill 2408. The bill aimed to create a "Cyber Code," but was ultimately defeated on the House floor in April 2010. The House Resolution 545, which calls for an investigation into the need for the Police cybercrime division to receive additional funding, is currently under review by the House's Internal Affairs Committee: http://www.caribbeanbusinesspr.com/pmt_ed/puerto-rico-among-the-top-10-cyberattack-targets-globally-10680.html	One - Polytechnic University of Puerto Rico http://www.pupr.edu/information-assurance-and-security/	One university.	None.	Microsoft, Cisco, Oracle, Hewlett-Packard have operations in Puerto Rico. Infotech Aerospace Services (IAS), Honeywell Aerospace, Lockheed Martin, Pratt & Whitney and Hamilton Sunstrand are also present: http://www.pridco.com/industries/Pages/Information-Technology.aspx	In 2014 the NSF's grant No. DUE-1438838 funded the University of Puerto Rico-Rio Piedras with $299,982 to advance cybersecurity knowledge in Puerto Rico. "This project, at the University of Puerto Rico-Rio Piedras, is the first step in creating a research, development, and education program in cybersecurity at the institution." http://ccom.uprrp.edu/~atackpr/index.php?mact=News,cntnt01,detail,0&cntnt01articleid=4&cntnt01returnid=15	Relatively low.

CONCLUSIONS

Based on the resultant table we can divide all the states, depending on their level of cybersecurity development, into six categories, from "Excellent" to "Low".

The first category, "Excellent", consists of two exceptional states: Maryland and Texas. Each of them has 16 CAEs, tens of universities and colleges offering cybersecurity programs of various levels, very serious cybersecurity facilities and research centers, dozens of powerful cybersecurity companies and government contractors.

The second category, "Very good", consists of four powerful states: California, Illinois, New York, and Pennsylvania. Each of them has seven or eight CAEs, prominent educational cybersecurity programs at university and college levels, leading cybersecurity research centers, many cybersecurity companies and governmental contractors, and a lot of funds granted to the local cybersecurity-related institutions.

The third category, "Good", consists of 11 states in which the level of cybersecurity development is good and can be considered as adequate taking into account these states' other parameters: Alabama, Colorado, DC, Florida, Massachusetts, Michigan, New Jersey, North Carolina, Ohio, Oklahoma, Virginia. Each of them has from four to seven CAEs, sufficient numbers of the academic programs in cybersecurity, related research centers, government contractors and cybersecurity-related companies.

The fourth, most populated, category is "Rather good". These 16 states have relatively good level of cybersecurity development, but, taking into account their potential, can do even better: Arizona, Connecticut, Georgia, Indiana, Kansas, Louisiana, Minnesota, Mississippi, Missouri, Nebraska, New Hampshire, New Mexico, Oregon, Tennessee, Utah and Washington. For example, some of them definitely can have more CAEs than they have currently: Arizona (3), New Mexico (2), Oregon (0), Utah (1), Washington (3).

The fifth category consists of 12 states where the level of cybersecurity development is relatively low, but they, at least, conduct visible efforts to improve the situation: Delaware, Hawaii, Idaho, Iowa, Maine, Montana, Nevada, Rhode Island, South Dakota, Vermont, West Virginia, Puerto Rico. If they will continue this positive trend, then can hope to move to the higher level of cybersecurity development rather soon.

Finally, the last category is "Low". It consists of seven states with the lowest level of cybersecurity development, and it looks that they are not making enough efforts to improve the situation: Alaska, Arkansas, Kentucky, North Dakota, South Carolina, Wisconsin and Wyoming. For example, altogether these seven states have only four CAEs, while four of them don't have CAEs at all.

Overall, we can come to the conclusion that, under the current difficult global cybersecurity situation, when powerful adversarial to the USA nations rapidly develop their cybersecurity potential, majority of the American united states underperform in the cybersecurity area. Specifically, we need more and better prepared human resources to be ready to withstand those global threats. More cybersecurity educational programs with courses specifically targeting those global menaces should be developed and funded in our country. Only in such a way we will prepare adequate number of cyber warriors familiar enough with our potential global enemies and their cybersecurity capabilities, tactics and strategies.

BIBLIOGRAPHY

[1] Arati Prabhakar, DirectorDefense Advanced Projects Research Agency, Defense One Conference, November 2014

[2] Keith B. Alexander, The Next Wave Introduction, NSA/CSS website, 2012, https://www.nsa.gov/research/tnw/tnw194/article2.shtml

[3] James Clapper, Intel Heads Now Fear Cyber Attack More Than Terror, Quote to Congressional Testimony, March 2013

200+ DHS/NSA Centers of Academic Excellence exist across the United States at various colleges and universities, mostly concentrated around the Beltway, the East Coast seaboard through Texas. While these have been engines of dissemination for emerging government standards for cybersecurity education and workforce development (NIST/NICE initiative), there are thousands of universities and colleges that are not aboard and are graduating students with an unawareness of cybersecurity.

[4] Tripwire, Cyber Security Tops Intelligence Community's 2014 Threat Assessment, Feb 10, 2014

[5] InfoSec Institute, Cyber Threat Analysis, http://resources.infosecinstitute.com/cyber-threat-analysis/

[6] David Bisson, NSA Chief Concerned about Cyber Attacks on U.S. Critical Infrastructure, Wired Magazine, 21 November 2014.

[7] John A. Van Messel, Unrestricted Warfare: A Chinese doctrine for future warfare. Marine Corps University, June 2005

[8] Mark A. Stokes, Jenny Lin and L.C. Russell Hsiao; The Chinese People's Liberation Army Signals Intelligence and Cyber Reconnaissance Infrastructure; Project 2049 Institute; November 11, 2011

[9] "Cyber Security Dictionary". 2 Jan 2012. Retrieved 23 March 2014.

[10] Walt Boys, "Back to Basics: SCADA", Automation TV: Control Global - Control Design, 18 August 2009.

[11] Anshul Thakur, SCADA, Engineering Garage, http://www.engineersgarage.com/articles/scada-systems.

[12] Eric Byres, SCADA security Basics: SCADA VS ICS terminology, Tofino Security, 5 September 2012 (https://www.tofinosecurity.com/blog/scada-security-basics-scada-vs-ics-terminology)

[13] Anshul Thakur, SCADA, Engineering Garage, http://www.engineersgarage.com/articles/scada-systems

[14] Arati Prabhakar, Director, Defense Advanced Projects Research Agency, Defense One Conference, November 2014

[15] United States Government Accountability Office. Cyber Security, National Strategy, Roles, and Responsibilities Need to Be Better Defined and More Effectively Implemented. GAO. February 2013

[16] Martin C. Libicki, David Senty, Julia Pollack. Hackers Wanted, An Examination of the Cyber Security Labor Market, RAND. June 18, 2014
[17a] probability of 1

[17] US Cyber Command, Cyber Mission Force Operation Plan (unclassified briefing)

[18] United States Government Accountability Office. Cyber Security, National Strategy, Roles, and Responsibilities Need to Be Better Defined and More Effectively Implemented. GAO. February 2013

[19] Martin C. Libicki, David Senty, Julia Pollack. Hackers Wanted, An Examination of the Cyber Security Labor Market, RAND. June 18, 2014.

Appendix: State by State Detailed Reports

ALABAMA

Alabama surprisingly has a large academic focus on cybersecurity with seven NSA/DHS-designated Centers of Academic Excellence—three of which have received SFS grants. There are a number of government contractors in the state, and the academic institutions/research centers collaborate with industry and military/government.

State / Policy Activities

Main cybersecurity page for the state

- http://www.cybersecurity.alabama.gov/

State Information Security Policy

- http://cybersecurity.alabama.gov/documents/Policy_600_Information_Security.pdf

Centers / Facilities

Auburn Cyber Research Center

- http://www.eng.auburn.edu/research/centers/auburn-cyber-research-center/index.html
- Research center within the Samuel Ginn College of Engineering at Auburn University.

Center for Information Security and Assurance

- http://www.jsu.edu/mcis/cisa/
- Research center at Jacksonville State University

Center of Information Assurance Education (CIAE)

- http://www.tuskegee.edu/academics/colleges/cbis/computer_science/ciae.aspx
- Located at Tuskegee University, serves as organizing body to offer resources and assistance for faculty, students, and community in conducting teaching, research, and other activities in Information Assurance.

Center for Forensics, Information Technology, and Security

- http://www.usacfits.org/
- At the University of South Alabama. Research and educational center dedicated to the collection and dissemination of information related to digital forensics and information technology assurance and security. Also collaborates with industry.

Universities

Auburn University

- CAE/IAE, CAE/R
- The college has a large "Cyber Initiative" including the OSINT lab and Cyber Research Center
    - http://www.aucyber.com/
- The Samuel Ginn College of Engineering offers a number of undergraduate and graduate degrees within which students can focus on cybersecurity through research centers and labs
    - http://www.eng.auburn.edu/

Jacksonville State University

- CAE/IAE

- http://www.jsu.edu/mcis/programs.html
- Offers programs in their Mathematical, Computing, & Information Sciences department with research in cybersecurity conducted though the Center for Information Security and Assurance.

Tuskegee University

- CAE/IAE
- Offers a Master of Science in Information Systems and Security Management
    - http://www.tuskegee.edu/academics/colleges/cbis/computer_science/graduate_program.aspx
- Cybersecurity education is coordinated through the Center of Information Assurance Education

Snead State Community College

- CAE/2Y
- http://www.snead.edu/about_us/college_departments/academic/technology.aspx
- The Technology Division offers Associates in Applied Science degrees and certificates in Computer Science Technology and Electronic Engineering Technology. The CST program offers an AAS Computer Science degree which includes courses in Cisco networking, network security, programming and database administration.

The University of Alabama at Birmingham

- CAE/R
- http://catalog.uab.edu/graduate/collegeofartsciences/interdisciplinaryprograms/computer-forensics-security-management/

- Offers a Master of Computer Forensics and Security Management program. Also offers a BS in Computer Science with a Computer Networking Specialization that includes security coursework.

University of Alabama Huntsville

- CAE/IAE
- http://www.uah.edu/science/departments/computer-science/graduate-students/graduate-degree-programs
- Offers a Master of Science in Cybersecurity through the Computer Science department

University of South Alabama

- CAE/IAE
- http://cyb.soc.southalabama.edu/
- School of Computing offers a Cyber Assurance specialization. Also has the Center for Forensics, Information Technology, and Security.

Wallace State Community College

- http://www.wallacestate.edu/Programs/Alphabetic-Listing-of-Departments/index
- Offers a Cybersecurity/Computer Forensics specialization within the Computer Science AAS and Criminal Justice AAS degree programs.

Troy University

- http://www.troy.edu/college-of-arts-and-sciences/cybersecurity.html
- Offers a cybersecurity focus within the College of Arts & Sciences

Companies

- Northrop Grumman
- Quantum Research International, Inc.
- Boeing
- Sentar, Inc.
- Boecore
- MEI Technologies
- Integration Innovation, Inc.
- Booz Allen Hamilton
- NHR Global
- Davidson Technologies, Inc.
- Radiance Technologies, Inc.
- SAIC
- Torch Technologies

Funding

- NSF Scholarship for Service grants awarded to three colleges in Alabama

ALASKA

Alaska has one designated CAE. Not very much going on in this state.

State / Policy Activities

Alaska's DoA Security website, with links:

- http://doa.alaska.gov/ets/security/

The State of Alaska was fined $1.7 million for a security breach in 2012:

- http://www.securitymagazine.com/articles/83272-state-of-alaska-fined--1-7-million-for-security-breach-

Centers / Facilities

Advanced System Security Education, Research, and Training Center (ASSERT)

- http://assert.uaf.edu/
- A multidisciplinary center located at the University of Alaska Fairbanks. The center provides curriculum development, program development, workshops, research opportunities, K-12 outreach, and access to IA research resources.

Universities

University of Alaska Fairbanks

- CAE/IAE
- https://www.cs.uaf.edu/
- College of Engineering and Mines offers undergraduate and graduate Computer Science majors.

- ASSERT research center is located here along with three ASSERT labs:
    - ASSERT Remote Access Lab
    - ASSERT Digital Forensics Lab
    - ASSERT SCADA Lab

Charter College

- http://www.chartercollege.edu/locations/anchorage-ak
- Has two campuses in Alaska. Offers AAS and certificate programs in Network Security

Companies

- Rolling Bay, LLC
- Siemens
- CTG
- Progressive IT
- Alaska Communications Systems
- NANA WorleyParsons, LLC
- CyberData Technologies
- General Dynamics - IT
- Leidos
- GCI
- NCR
- AT&T

Funding

None found

ARIZONA

Three Arizona Universities are NSA/DHS-designated CAEs, two of which receive SFS. Other NSF grants have also been awarded to University of Arizona, including the AZSecurity Cybersecurity Fellowship program. Arizona has a number of private security companies as well as government contractors who are researching cybersecurity, but there doesn't seem to be much information on state-level initiatives.

State / Policy Activities

Law/policy-wise I couldn't find much. There does not appear to be any state-level cybersecurity policy websites for Arizona as there are with several other states.

Business-wise: "Arizona is growing a "Cybersecurity Valley" with professionals in the public and private sector. Arizona State University has a budding Information Assurance Center, and schools such as the University of Advancing Technology in Tempe produce recruits for clandestine agencies of the U.S. government along with feeding cybersecurity firms with young talent. For a variety of reasons, which include the high-tech environment, existing defense contractors and a rare blend of Google-style culture in existing firms, some of the brightest cybersecurity talent is drawn to the Valley. The talent is attracted by boutique firms like Bishop Fox and Securosis, in part, because they protect many of the Fortune 100 and because the firms recognize and appreciate the inclinations for working odd hours from strange locations like the couch and the café. Even large companies such as Honeywell, Charles Schwab, American Express and Securosis have some or all their security teams based in the Valley, while other research firms like ARTIS work to understand human and state behavior related to cyberwarfare."

- http://www.azcentral.com/opinions/articles/20130708cybersecurity-valley-viewpoints.html

Centers / Facilities

Laboratory of Security Engineering for Future Computing (SEFCOM)

- http://sefcom.asu.edu/
- The mission of SEFCOM at Arizona State University is to make significant impact to our society through innovative research projects, assurable development, and hands-on training programs in the areas of cyberspace security and defense. Current research interests include identity management and access control, formal models for computer security, network and distributed systems security including mobile and cloud computing, vulnerability and risk assessment and cyber crime analysis among others.

Information Assurance Center

- http://ia.asu.edu/
- At Arizona State University. A University-wide center based in the School of Computing, Informatics, and Decision System Engineering of Ira A. Fulton School of Engineering at ASU, with faculty participants from Arts and sciences, Business, Engineering, Public Policy, Technology and Innovation. The center emphasizes on research and education in the increasingly important multi-disciplinary fields, including subjects ranging from science and engineering to management, public policy and social sciences.

ARTIS Research – Cyber Behavior and Defense (CBAD) Institute

- http://artisresearch.com/center-for-cyber-defense/
- ARTIS research is headquartered in Arizona. Their CBAD Institute brings together top technical, engineering, behavioral and security talent to better understand the three main components of cyber security: hardware, software and wetware (the human brain and its logical, psychological and social networking capabilities).

Universities

Arizona State University

- CAE/IAE, CAE/R
- http://ia.asu.edu/education.php
- Offers cybersecurity concentrations through the Information Assurance Center. The Information Assurance (IA) educational activities at ASU include the IA Concentration in five degree programs: B.S degree in computer science, B.S.E degree in computer systems engineering, M.S. and M.C.S degrees in computer science, and Ph.D. degree in computer science. The IA courseware has been certified by the Information Assurance Courseware Evaluation (IACE) Program to satisfy the standards for (1) Information Systems Security (INFOSEC) Professionals (NSTISSI 4011) and (2) Senior Systems Managers (CNSSI 4012).

University of Advancing Technology

- CAE/IAE
- Offers a Network Security BS degree and a Technology Forensics BS degree
    - http://www.uat.edu/network-security-degree/
    - http://majors.uat.edu/tech-forensics/

University of Arizona, Tucson

- CAE/IAE
- Eller College of Management offers an "AZSecure Cybersecurity Fellowship Program" within their Management Information Systems program
    - http://mis.eller.arizona.edu/AZSecure/index.asp

- Has a research focus in Aerospace/Defense/Homeland Security including cyber security
    - http://www.arizona.edu/information/corporations-businesses/aerospace-defense-homeland-security

Companies

- Bishop Fox
- Securosis
- TASC
- Honeywell
- ARTIS Research
- Defense Point Security
- CGI
- Mitre Corporation
- STG, Inc.
- Raytheon
- TechUSA
- Ukpeagvik Inupiat Corporation
- URS Corporation
- ITT Educational Services Inc.
- Leidos
- USIS
- Western Refining
- BeyondTrust
- General Dynamics C4 Systems
- NHR Global
- Booz Allen Hamilton
- SAIC
- Jacobs Technology
- NCI Information Systems, In

Funding

- $5.4M In Cybersecurity Grants Awarded To University Of Arizona Researchers by NSF
- http://www.darkreading.com/risk/$54m-in-cybersecurity-grants-awarded-to-university-of-arizona-researchers/d/d-id/1140584?

- NSF Scholarship for Service grants awarded to two Arizona Universities
- NSF AZSecurity Cybersecurity Fellowship grant awarded to University of Arizona

Other Notations

The Arizona Technology Council

- http://www.aztechcouncil.org/
- An Arizona trade association for science and technology companies. The Arizona Technology Council offers numerous events, educational forums and business conferences that bring together leaders, managers, employees and visionaries to make an impact on the technology industry.

ARKANSAS

Arkansas has two NSA/DHS-designated Centers of Academic Excellence. I didn't find very many security companies here. The AR state government seems to promote cybersecurity transparency and education online more than some others.

State / Policy Activities

Arkansas state government has a couple websites outlining cyber policies and providing residents with cyber resources/education. The state government promotes cybersecurity awareness through their sites and observing events such as "National Preparedness Month."

Arkansas State Department of Information Systems (DIS) Cyber Security site:

- http://www.dis.arkansas.gov/security/Pages/default.aspx

Arkansas Department of Education Cyber Safety Resources site:

- http://www.arkansased.org/divisions/learning-services/technology-initiatives-and-resources/cyber-safety-resources

Centers / Facilities

Center for Information Security & Reliability

- http://isr.csce.uark.edu/
- At the University of Arkansas. The activities of this center includes, but not limited to the following: fostering multidisciplinary research, securing large-scale funding from federal, state, and other funding agencies, providing education and training to future work-force, increasing awareness in the field of

information security and reliability by offering appropriate seminars and workshops.

Center for Excellence for Assurance, Security, and Software Usability, Research, and Education (ASSURE)

- http://ualr.edu/computerscience/assure/
- At the University of Arkansas at Little Rock. The ASSURE Center at UALR serves as an organizing body to centralize the education and research efforts of faculty pursuing research and education in information assurance, security, and software usability.

Universities

University of Arkansas

- CAE/R
- The Computer Science and Engineering department offers undergraduate and graduate degrees that allow for security research and education.
    - http://www.csce.uark.edu/
- The Center for Information Security & Reliability is located here and houses three different security-based labs for student research:
    - The Database Security Research Lab: http://isr.csce.uark.edu/labnew.html
    - The RFID INFOSEC Lab: http://rfidsecurity.uark.edu/
    - The Trustable Logic Circuit Design Lab: http://comp.uark.edu/~jdi/Research_new.htm

University of Arkansas at Little Rock

- CAE/IAE

- http://ualr.edu/computerscience/
- Offers Information Assurance research specializations through undergraduate and graduate Computer Science programs. The ASSURE Center is located here and coordinates research and education in Information Assurance.

University of Arkansas Community College Batesville

- http://www.uaccb.edu/academics/academic-divisions/business-technology-public-service/cyber-security
- UACCB supports the incorporation of Cyber Security into the technology curriculum. The college also provides support for advancing security awareness through annual events for middle school students and a Cyber Security Summit for the community.

Companies

- AT&T
- Aerojet Rocketdyne
- Ukpeagvik Inupiat Corporation
- General Dynamics - IT
- QualChoice

CALIFORNIA

California envisions their state as a leader in cybersecurity innovation. The state has a robust legislative framework related to information security with some of the earliest data breach laws on the books. The state government engages in cyber awareness exercises and has a cross-sector cybersecurity working group focused on improving the state's posture against security threats and vulnerabilities. California has an enormous academic infrastructure with well over a dozen programs tailored towards cybersecurity education in a number of narrowed specialized. The state is home to seven NSA Centers of Academic Excellence and is home to multiple cybersecurity focused research and development centers. The state is home not only to the major Silicon Valley companies but also hundreds of small start-ups, niche market companies, and boutique firms providing cybersecurity services to the nation's largest state economy.

State / Policy Activities

California envisions their state as a leader in cybersecurity innovation. The state has a robust legislative framework related to information security with some of the earliest data breach laws on the books. The state government engages in cyber awareness exercises and has a cross-sector cybersecurity working group focused on improving the state's posture against security threats and vulnerabilities. California has an enormous academic infrastructure with well over a dozen programs tailored towards cybersecurity education in a number of narrowed specialized. The state is home to seven NSA Centers of Academic Excellence and is home to multiple cybersecurity focused research and development centers. The state is home not only to the major Silicon Valley companies but also hundreds of small start-ups, niche market companies, and boutique firms providing cybersecurity services to the nation's largest state economy.

Centers / Facilities

California has many research centers, facilities, and national laboratories working in the cybersecurity field. Particularly there is a high concentration of Federally Funded Research and Development Centers (FFRDCs) such as the Jet Propulsion Laboratory, the Aerospace Corporation, Sandia National Labs – California location, Lawrence Livermore National Laboratory, the RAND Corporation, and a variety of military and security facilities.

Universities

California has among the largest university systems in America. There are well over a dozen major universities offering specializations in cybersecurity education. Many of the state's largest and most elite schools have specialized centers and laboratories devoted to information security studies.

- Center for Computer Systems Security – USC
- Center for Information Assurance and Security – Cal State University, Sacramento
- San Jose State University
- Berkeley (multiple centers out of their EE/CS department)
- Cyber Security for Information Assurance and Security Management – Cal State University San Bernardino
- Secure Computing & Network Center (SCONCE) – University of California Irvine
- Naval Postgraduate School Center for Information Systems Security Studies and Research (NPS CISR) – Monterey, California
- Cal State Polytechnic
- University of California Davis
- UCLA – Center for Encrypted Functionalities

Additionally, the state is home to seven NSA Centers of Academic Excellence supplementing the state's other well-known and recognized intellectual centers like Stanford, Berkeley and UCLA.

Companies

Silicon Valley provides an enormous industrial base for cybersecurity advancement and heavily recruits California's information security talent directly out of the state's large university base. Silicon Valley tech companies with specialized security departments include Google, Apple, Facebook, Adobe, LinkedIn, HP, Rackspace, and many others. In addition to the many tech giants there are also hundreds of niche and boutique information security companies that develop software, build hardware, and provide consulting services on security.

Other Notations

California's size and breadth allows their cybersecurity institutions to focus on many topics. Particularly important appears to energy grid security, cryptography, secure software development, and high performance computing. The state's institutions draw funding the NSF, DoD, NASA, and many other federal grant providing agencies. The companies that make up the high tech sector also offer rich opportunities for funding and research grants.

1) Legislation at the state level in the area of cybersecurity.

- California was the first state to enact a data security breach notification law with SB 1386 in 2003, the law has been the de facto model adopted around the country for state level breach laws. The law covers personal information and later expanded to include medical/health-care information.

- Around 2006, state law allowed for the creation of the Office of the State Chief Information Officer (OCIO). In 2009, the Office was expanded and reorganized consolidating a number of groups that managed information security, procurements and other IT related functions for the state. In 2010, the OCIO was renamed the California Technology Agency (CTA).

- At present, California's cybersecurity efforts are coordinated out of the Office of Information Security (OIS) under the CTA or Department of Technology.

- The California Office of Information Security has responsibility and authority over statewide information security and privacy policies, and standards applicable to all state government agencies, as outlined in Government Code Section 11549, Chapter 183, of the Statutes of 2007 (Senate Bill 90).

- California drafts and publishes an annual IT Strategic Plan and for 2014 their fourth goal is to "Secure and Manage Information as an Asset."

- Their security goals include most of the basic things expected like compliance implementation and management, raise awareness and educate state employees and residents, and implement next-generation security tools. There is also a focus on leveraging state data by using analytics with goals to enable better transparency, information sharing, and shared capabilities and collaboration. They maintain a desire to employ data management and collaboration tools to make data analysis easier and increase the value of collected data.

- The California OIS also hosts an Annual Cyber Security Awareness Event with participants from the advisory board including state and local government authorities, academics, and critical infrastructure operators.

- The OIS also established and chairs the California Cyber Security Task Force which has seven sub-committees focusing on the following areas to advance California's state cyber security programs.
    o Legislation and Funding

- o Cyber-Emergency Preparedness
- o Risk Mitigation
- o Information Sharing
- o Cyber-Security Workforce Development
- o High-tech and Digital Forensics
- o Economic Development
- 2013 Cyber Laws Expanded
    - o California law already imposes a requirement to provide notice to affected customers of unauthorized access to, or disclosure of, personal information in certain circumstances. S.B. 46 adds to the current data security breach notification requirements a new category of data triggering these notification requirements: A user name or email address, in combination with a password or security question and answer that would permit access to an online account.
    - o A.B. 370 amends the California Online Privacy Protection Act (CalOPPA) to require companies that collect personally identifiable information online to include information about how they respond to "do not track" signals, as well as other information about their collection and use of personally identifiable information. The newly required information includes:
        - How the company responds to "do not track" signals or other mechanisms that provide consumers the ability to exercise choice over the collection of personally identifiable information about their online activities over time and across third-party websites or online services, if the company collects such information; and

- Whether third parties may collect personally identifiable information about a consumer's online activities over time and across different websites when a consumer uses the company's website.

- Other California cybersecurity and privacy law resources:
    - http://www.cio.ca.gov/OIS/Government/library/laws_regs.asp
- California DOJ Information regarding security breaches with a catalog of previous breach disclosures:
    - http://oag.ca.gov/ecrime/databreach/list
- Attorney General Kamala D. Harris established the eCrime Unit in 2011. The eCrime Unit is tasked with investigating and prosecuting large scale identity theft and technology crimes with actual losses in excess of $50,000.
    - The primary mission of the eCrime Unit is to investigate and prosecute multi-jurisdictional criminal organizations, networks, and groups that perpetrate identity theft crimes, use an electronic device or network to facilitate a crime, or commit a crime targeting an electronic device, network or intellectual property.
    - provides investigative and prosecutorial support to the five California regional high-tech task forces funded through the High Technology Theft Apprehension and Prosecution (HTTAP) Program Trust Fund
- California DOJ also robust system for identity theft remediation and information as part of the above mentioned program and also provides a centralized state resources for making Internet based criminal complaints
- State Administrative Manual for California's information security policies and guidelines http://sam.dgs.ca.gov/TOC/5300.aspx

- Office of the Attorney General cybersecurity page - https://oag.ca.gov/cybersecurity

2) Centers of cybersecurity research/practice.
    - Academia
        - Center for Computer Systems Security – USC
        - Center for Information Assurance and Security – Cal State University, Sacramento
        - San Jose State University
        - Berkeley (multiple centers out of their EE/CS department)
        - Cyber Security for Information Assurance and Security Management – Cal State University San Bernardino
        - Secure Computing & Network Center (SCONCE) – University of California Irvine
        - Naval Postgraduate School Center for Information Systems Security Studies and Research (NPS CISR) – Monterey, California
        - Cal State Polytechnic
        - Cal Davis
        - UCLA – Center for Encrypted Functionalities
    - Private Sector
        - Google, Apple, Adobe, etc.
        - Tons of smaller niche and boutique security firms
    - Government/Federally Funded Research and Development Centers
        - The Aerospace Corporation
        - RAND Corporation

- Lawrence Livermore
- JPL
- Sandia National Laboratories (California location)
- Various Military installations

3) Technical/analytical cybersecurity facilities in the state.
   - See FFRDC list above

4) What are the state's cybersecurity main research/practice focus(es).
   - Cryptography, Energy Grid security, eCrime, software development

5) What funding do they have from the funding agencies (NSF, etc.).
   - 7 distinct CAE's in California
   - University funding coming from NSF, DoD, DoE, and other
   - Grants from cash flushed tech companies/silicon valley firms

COLORADO

Colorado has 5 NSA-designated CAEs. They also offer a number of online degree programs with focus in cybersecurity through Colorado State University's "Global" online campus. There is a large number of contractors and military presence focusing on cyber security in Colorado, including the Air Force Academy and their associated cyber research center. Colorado Springs was named one of the "Top 5 Cities for Cyber Security Jobs" by clearancejobs.com;

Link: http://news.clearancejobs.com/2013/05/23/top-5-cities-for-cyber-security-jobs/

State / Policy Activities

Colorado Office of Information Security (OIS)

- http://www.colorado.gov/cs/Satellite/OIT-Cyber/CBON/1249667675596
- The Colorado Office of Information Security is a unit within the Governor's Office of Information Technology and is the single state source for cyber security readiness and awareness. OIS is directly aligned with the goals and objectives of the National Strategy to Secure Cyberspace. Working closely with federal, state, local and private sector partners, the Office of Information Security actively gathers and analyzes information on cyber threats and vulnerabilities that present risk to the state's information systems or the critical information managed within.

State Information Security Policies

- http://www.colorado.gov/cs/Satellite/OIT-Cyber/CBON/1251575408771

Centers / Facilities

US Air Force Academy Center for Cyberspace Research (ACCR)

- http://www.usafa.edu/df/dfe/dfer/centers/accr/
- Mission is to enhance cadet education through research in the domain of Cyberspace. Center participates in cyber defense competitions as well as research, education, and awareness-building initiatives.

Lockheed Martin "Security Intelligence Center" – Denver

- http://www.lockheedmartin.com/us/what-we-do/information-technology/cyber-security/security-intelligence-center.html
- One of two Lockheed Martin SICs in the US (the other being in Maryland). The centers are operated by Lockheed's Computer Incident Response Team. They are staffed by cyber-intelligence analysts who "identify patterns of persistent campaigns spanning multiple attacks, and implementing new mitigations to get ahead of the threats."
    - http://www.spacecolorado.org/news/lockheed-martin-opens-denver-security-center.html

Colorado Research Institute for Security and Privacy (CRISP)

- http://crisp.cs.du.edu/
- An active research group in information security and privacy at the Department of Computer Science of the University of Denver. CRISP is dedicated to creating tools and techniques that is directly useful for a broad audience, going beyond the usual construction of academic proof-of-concept prototypes.

Cyber Research Facility

- http://www.uccs.edu/cs/research/cybersecurity/cyberresearchfacility.html
- Located at the University of Colorado, Colorado Springs. Aside from being an educational hub for cybersecurity at the university, the center contains an "innovation security lab" to foster development of educational and research programs in Cyber Security, Physical Security, and Homeland Security.

Universities

Colorado Technical University

- CAE/IAE
- Offers a number of undergraduate and graduate degrees focusing on cybersecurity from different perspectives through four different departments: Computer Science, Engineering, Homeland Security, and Information Technology.
- Degrees Include:
    - BS in Cybercrime Investigation
        - http://www.coloradotech.edu/degrees/bachelors/cybercrime-investigation
    - BS in Cyber Security which offers two concentrations: Computer Systems Security and Information Assurance.
        - http://www.coloradotech.edu/degrees/bachelors/cyber-security
    - Master of Science in Homeland Security, with a Cybersecurity Policy concentration
        - http://www.coloradotech.edu/degrees/masters/homeland-security/cybersecurity

Regis University

- CAE/IAE
- Offers graduate-level cybersecurity education through an MS in Information Assurance degree with an optional Cyber Security specialization, and a graduate certificate in Cyber Security.
    - o http://regis.edu/CPS/Academics/Degrees-and-Programs/Graduate-Programs/MS-Information-Assurance.aspx
    - o http://informationassurance.regis.edu/ia-programs/ms-ia-cyber-security-grad-certificate

United States Air Force Academy

- CAE/IAE
- Offers three computer science degrees with courses ad research options in cybersecurity. Also has the Center for Cyberspace Research.
    - o http://www.usafa.edu/df/dfcs/dfcs/Majors.cfm

University of Colorado, Colorado Springs

- CAE/IAE
- http://eas.uccs.edu/cs/cyberSecurity.shtml
- The university offers a number of degrees and specializations in cybersecurity through their Computer Science department. They offer a focus in IA through their Master of Engineering degree and a concentration in security through their PhD in Engineering degree program.
- Also has the Cyber Research Facility.

University of Denver

- CAE/IAE
- Offers an Information Security Master's degree
    - http://universitycollege.du.edu/smgt/degree/masters/information-security-online/degreeid/431
- Also offers an Information Systems Security Master's degree
    - http://universitycollege.du.edu/ict/degree/masters/information-systems-security-online/degreeid/402
- Also has CRISP center for cybersecurity research.

Colorado State University Global (CSU Global)

- Offers online degree programs, including cyber security degree specializations and certification programs. Also offers a Master's degree in Information Technology Management with an optional cyber security specialization.
    - https://csuglobal.edu/undergraduate/programs/certificates-completion/cyber-security/
    - https://csuglobal.edu/graduate/programs/masters-degrees/information-technology-management/

Companies

- Security Pursuit
- Denver Cyber Security
- Northrop Grumman
- Lockheed Martin
- Tyco
- TASC
- Novetta Solutions
- Veredus Corporation
- CRGT Inc.
- Entegee
- CenturyLink
- Ayda Labs Inc.

- Booz Allen Hamilton
- Syntelligent Analytic Solutions, LLC
- Vencore
- USfalcon
- L-3 Communications
- Global Technology Resources, Inc.
- Raytheon Canada Ltd.
- Raytheon
- Coalfire Systems
- Kingfisher Systems

Funding

- 1.25 Million AFOSR equipment grant given to UC Colorado Springs for the Cyber Research Facility

CONNECTICUT

Connecticut is proud of the work they are doing to be the first state to present a unified cyber security utilities response plan with the Public Utilities Regulatory Authority (PURA). They are working to integrate their activities with DHS.

State / Policy Activities

This April CT's governor released the thirty-one page State Cybersecurity Strategy integrating PURA to work on a cybersecurity strategy in partnership with all public utilities. CT claims to be the first state to present a unified plan and will share this with other states. The state has a Cyber security resource page Welcome to CT.Gov/Cybersafe and passed a cyber bullying law in 2013.

Governor 2013 Comprehensive Energy Strategy for Connecticut – 2013 – strategy to protect electrical grid.

http://www.ct.gov/occ/lib/occ/11.22.13lauren.pdf

Centers / Facilities

UCONN – the state's only Center for Academic Excellence and Research

- Center for Hardware Assurance, Security, and Engineering – Center for Excellence for Security Innovation, created a cybersecurity research program underwritten by Comcast (Millions of $$ over three years)

- UCONN Tech Park $162.3 million investment. state-of-the-art facility for advancing the competitiveness of Connecticut industry, and for the economic success of our state

- Six professors and seven doctoral candidates will work at the center, which will be in the Information Technologies Engineering building on UConn's main campus. Mark

Tehranipoor, the director of the partnership, said his goal is to make the center "a national authority for hardware, software and network security."

Universities

Universities, community colleges and technical institutes offering degrees or certificates:

- CharterOak State College
- Quinebaug Valley Community College
- Sacred Heart University Certificate Program in Cybersecurity
- New England Institute of Technology
- Ridley-Lowell Business & Technical Institute
- University of Connecticut / Engineering and School of Business
- ITT
- Norwalk Community College University of New Haven – Network Systems MS
- Southern Connecticut State University
- DeVry

Companies

- Comcast (invested in CONN Tech Park)
- Pratt & Whitney ($9 million investment) in the UCONN center
- Essilor of America
- Hartman International
- Continental Resources
- GLN
- Datto, Inc
- OpenSky Corp
- Open Systems Technologies
- USIS
- A. Global Engineering

- Alta Vision Systems LLC
- Connecticut Computer Network Security and Disaster Recovery
- Wellington Steele & Associates
- RSB Securities

Funding

- DoD - $75 million?
- $2 million in Fed grants (2012) NCAEIAR – John Chandy

Other Notations

1) Investing in the power grid 2013 to put cyber security into state's energy strategy.

2) 4/14/2014 – CT Cybersecurity Strategy with Utilities Public Utilities Regulatory Authority (PURA) - Connecticut is the first state to present a cybersecurity strategy in partnership with the utilities, and will share it with other states working on similar plans. http://www.governor.ct.gov/malloy/cwp/view.asp?Q=543324&A=4010

DISTRICT OF COLUMBIA

DC currently has 5 NSA/DHS-designated academic Centers of Excellence, one of which offers an SFS scholarship. DC obviously has the federal government presence, which has recently been pushing for more and more cybersecurity positions and education. This push has surely attracted cybersecurity researchers and companies to the DC metro area, while virtually all of the academic institutions in the greater DC area (including North VA and MD) now offer cybersecurity-related curricula. DC is fast becoming a hot bed of cybersecurity jobs.

State / Policy Activities

GSA is pushing for the establishment of a civilian cybersecurity center in the DC area

- http://www.bizjournals.com/washington/breaking_ground/2014/03/gsa-justice-to-study-civilian-cyber.html?page=all

DC proper may not have a real glut of cybersecurity companies / institutions aside from the federal presence and the federal emphasis on cybersecurity—as the greater area (VA/MD) has much of the firms. There is definitely an attraction for companies to set up shop in the greater DC metro area where they can market themselves towards the government as well as the private sector. Maryland and Virginia have gone so far as to attract cybersecurity contractors to their states using tax incentives. In 2013, Maryland Gov. Martin O'Malley announced over $3 million in tax breaks for cybersecurity companies in his state. Virginia has done similarly, establishing technology centers across the state with tax incentives including in the D.C. suburb of Arlington, Va.

- http://www.thehoya.com/dc-newest-hub-for-cybersecurity/

Evidence shows that the DC metro area is being "remade into the federal government's hub for cybersecurity work." Statistics show DC as having the most cybersecurity job listings in the country.

- http://www.washingtonpost.com/news/capital-business/wp/2014/03/05/evidence-that-the-d-c-area-really-is-a-hotbed-for-cybersecurity-jobs/

Centers / Facilities

The Center for Strategic and International Studies (CSIS)

- http://csis.org/category/topics/technology/cybersecurity
- CSIS is a bipartisan, nonprofit organization headquartered in Washington, D.C. The Center's 220 full-time staff and large network of affiliated scholars conduct research and analysis and develop policy initiatives that look to the future and anticipate change.
- CSIS focuses on many topics, including technology and cybersecurity through the Strategic Technologies Program.

The Brookings Institution

- http://www.brookings.edu/research/topics/cybersecurity
- "Think tank" organization. A nonprofit public policy organization based in Washington, DC. Our mission is to conduct high-quality, independent research and, based on that research, to provide innovative, practical recommendations that advance three broad goals: Strengthen American democracy; Foster the economic and social welfare, security and opportunity of all Americans; and Secure a more open, safe, prosperous and cooperative international system. Brookings experts research various aspects of cybersecurity and how to create a secure cyber environment.

The Cybersecurity and Policy Research Institute – GWU

- http://www.cspri.seas.gwu.edu/
- The Cyber Security Policy and Research Institute (CSPRI) is a center for GW and the Washington area to promote technical research and policy analysis of issues that have a significant computer security and information assurance component.

National Cybersecurity Institute – Excelsior College

- http://www.nationalcybersecurityinstitute.org/
- The National Cybersecurity Institute (NCI) is an academic and research center located in Washington D.C. dedicated to assisting government, industry, military, and academic sectors meet the challenges in cyber security policy, technology and education.

Universities

Howard University

- CAE/IAE
- http://www.howard.edu/csl/
- Courses and research in cybersecurity are offered through The Cybersecurity Education and Research Center, within the Department of Systems and Computer Science and the Department of Information Systems and Decision Sciences.

The George Washington University

- CAE/IAE, CAE/R
- http://www.cs.gwu.edu/academics/graduate_programs/master/cybersecurity
- Offers a MS degree in Cybersecurity and houses the Cybersecurity and Policy Research Institute

Georgetown University

- CAE/IAE
- Offers a cybersecurity strategy certificate program.
    - http://scs.georgetown.edu/programs_nc/CE0125/cybersecurity-strategy?dID=5
- The Georgetown Law School has a Cybersecurity Law Institute.
    - http://www.law.georgetown.edu/continuing-legal-education/programs/cle/cybersecurity/
- An Information Security track is offered through the Technology Management graduate program
    - http://scs.georgetown.edu/programs/77/master-of-professional-studies-in-technology-management#IS

The National Defense University (NDU) Information Resources Management College (iCollege)

- CAE/IAE
- http://icollege.ndu.edu/
- Offers a graduate-level cybersecurity program as well as several other cyber leadership/management programs.

The University of the District of Columbia

- CAE/IAE
- Has The Assurance Research Center for Trusted Information Computing (ARCTIC) which functions as a focal point for cybersecurity education at the university. Also offers a MS degree in Homeland Security.
    - http://informatics.udc.edu/arctic/
    - http://www.udc.edu/programs/homeland_security

Companies

- Most notably, of course, is the federal government and the military
- TASC
- L-3 Communications
- TDI
- CGRT
- Northrop Grumman
- Booz Allen Hamilton
- Six3 Systems
- Quantum Research International
- BAE Systems
- National Security Agency
- Noblis
- SRA International, Inc.
- Celestar Corporation
- General Dynamics - IT

Funding

- SFS grant awarded to George Washington University

DELAWARE

Delaware is extremely proactive in how it manages and cultivates cybersecurity. There are multiple broad collaborative efforts in progress that will increase the state's ability to secure not only its own assets but to provide talented young cybersecurity professionals to the federal government.

State / Policy Activities

Delaware has strong data protection laws covering personally identifiable information that lean heavily towards consumer protection. One of their most recent legislative efforts mandates that commercial entities take all reasonable steps to destroy personal information and the law outlines methods by which the destruction can be carried out. Interestingly, failures to destroy personal information that is then exposed can open commercial entities open to civil litigation or state directed administrative actions. Delaware is highly active in cybersecurity efforts targeting capacity generation and state level planning. Just this year the Governor announced the formation of the Delaware Cyber Initiative (DCI) with $3 million in funding. The initiative will build a collaborative cyber research network and create a laboratory in partnership with a number of the state's educational institutions. The lab will be built on the site of a former Chrysler plant and will operate similarly to a business park that's devoted to cyber innovation. The initiative will strive to train up a cadre of highly qualified cybersecurity students that can help fill domestic and federal gaps in security employment.

Delaware is also one of a number of states (Washington being the first) to leverage the capabilities of the state's National Guard for cybersecurity. There are also a number of non-traditional cyber recruiting and awareness projects residing in Delaware. For examples, the Cyber Aces program provides online testing and education and then selects the top scoring finalists to compete in rigorous highly modern competition. The state also plays hosts to a number of cyber challenges and summer boot camps for cyber students. Currently, there exists a NSF funded cybersecurity research initiative incorporating the University of Delaware and two of the state's community colleges. The initiative will increase course offerings and offer internships. Overall, Delaware is extremely progressive and pro-active in cybersecurity matters.

Centers / Facilities

Delaware lacks the research facility footprint found in many larger states. They have made efforts to involve their National Guard units and the Delaware Air Guard will be breaking ground on a new cyber facility in the future.

Universities

The state does have universities providing a variety of cybersecurity degree options and research foci. The state's major educational institutions are the University of Delaware and Delaware State University which both provided baccalaureate level opportunities for specializations in cybersecurity. Additionally, the state has involved its two-year colleges in recent cyber initiatives. The two major community colleges with cybersecurity learning opportunities are Delaware Technical Community College and Hartford Community College.

Other Notations

The state's cyber efforts are heavily oriented towards intellectual property protection and could generally be characterized as focused on corporate cybersecurity.

Delaware Supplemental Information

1) Legislation at the state level in the area of cybersecurity.
   - 2013 Delaware implemented state-wide cyberbullying policy with their DOE and DOJ

- July 2014 amended existing laws that mandate commercial entities to take all reasonable steps to destroy personal information of customers that is no longer being retained. Interestingly, the law exposes companies to civil lawsuits from consumers and administrative actions from the state DOJ. Makes it possible for consumers to seek damages via civil lawsuits.
- 2014 Delaware Cyber Initiative (DCI) being formed with an initial $3 million investment.
- The Delaware Cyber Initiative proposes $3 million for a collaborative learning and research network in the form of part research lab, part business park, dedicated to cyber innovation.
- The University of Delaware, Delaware State University, Delaware Technical Community College, and private institutions will develop the lab on the site of a former Chrysler assembly plant currently owned by the University of Delaware.
- The initiative will cater to large employers like Delaware's DuPont chemical company, but also to the state's banking and financial services sectors. Most important is that the initiative will allow government agencies to recruit cybersecurity professionals from the same pool available to private firms.
- The state has also recruited the Delaware National Guard as a resource for the DCI, part of a slow but growing trend among states and the federal government to deploy the National Guard to direct federal cyber resources to states.
- Regional Cybersecurity Initiative – UD, Delaware Technical CC, Hartford CC. Seeks to expand UD security course, create a security minor, transfer program for security students at CCs to transfer to UD programs, cyber internship program, middle and high school summer camps
- Cyber Aces Program – Governor sponsored talent identification program that provides online testing and education and then takes the top finalists and puts them in a competition simulating all-out

network warfare simulations. SANS involved and JP Morgan Chase.

- U.S. Cyber Challenge (USCC) will host its Summer Cyber Camp program in conjunction with the University of Delaware, Delaware State University, Wilmington University, Delaware Technical Community College and the Delaware Department of Technology and Information (DTI) from July 21-25, 2014. This will be the fifth consecutive year for the State of Delaware U.S. Cyber Challenge Summer Camp. The camp includes four days of intensive instruction by SANS instructors, a career fair, and a cyber-attack and defense competition with an awards ceremony to honor the winners. Invitation only based on performance in Cyber Quests challenges.

2) Centers of cybersecurity research/practice.

- University of Delaware Cybersecurity Initiative (UDCSI)
- DTCC Information Security Associate's Degree Program
- Wilmington University – certificates, bachelor's and master degree in information security related topics, CAE
- Delaware State University – Computer and Information Sciences has cyber curriculum

3) Technical/analytical cybersecurity facilities in the state.

- Delaware Air Guard
- PricewaterhouseCoopers
- Major Finance Sector companies like JP Morgan Chase
- DuPont
- Northrup Grumman

4) What are the state's cybersecurity main research/practice focus(es).

- State has a large focus on corporate information security via the importance of their financial sector companies, particularly JP Morgan Chase. Things like DLP, IP loss protection, etc.
- State's proximity to DC and the Beltway also brings focus on leadership, policy, and there's a huge focus on capacity generation.

5) What funding do they have from the funding agencies (NSF, etc.).

- Regional Cybersecurity Initiative funded by half million dollar NSF grant
- Otherwise no, it seems like
- Is actually getting some state tax money though.

FLORIDA

Florida is striving to become a national leader in cybersecurity education and research. There are already seven NSA-designated CAEs in the state, with many more colleges/universities offering cybersecurity and/or information assurance-focused curricula. The state has recently marked $5 million of their 2015 budget to fund a new state-wide Center for Cybersecurity, to be headquartered at the University of South Florida in Tampa. On top of this they have recently passed "sweeping legislation" tightening requirements for breach notification.

State / Policy Activities

Florida recently repealed its security breach law, and in its stead, passed "sweeping legislation" seen as possibly the broadest in the country. The set of bills impose tougher breach notification requirements on businesses, among other things, narrowing the breach notification period to 30 days; expanding the definition of person information to cover online login credentials that include username or email address used in conjunction with a password or security question; and compelling them to not only report, but to provide documentation and forensic reports, to the Attorney General's office on breaches affecting more than 500 Floridians. The law also requires that companies take "reasonable measures" to safeguard personal information in electronic form as well as dispose of customer records.

- From: http://www.scmagazine.com/fla-passes-sweeping-data-breach-notification-bill/article/357858/

A Board of Governors report requested by state legislature in 2013 focused on "Making Florida the Cyber State" by funding a Center for Cybersecurity and providing a "blueprint for Florida to develop cybersecurity as a central pillar of its economic future."

- Report can be found here: http://www.usf.edu/cybersecurity/documents/bogcybersecurityreport.pdf

For regional collaboration, Daytona State College is the lead institution in a consortium whose goal is to advance cyber forensic education in the southeastern United States. The consortium is comprised of nine colleges from Florida, Georgia and the Carolinas operating as the Southeastern Advanced Cybersecurity Education Consortium (ACE).

Centers / Facilities

Florida Center for Cybersecurity – University of South Florida, Tampa

- Still in development. Intended to be a large-scale hub for cybersecurity research and education, collaborating between universities, private industry, and government.
- http://www.usf.edu/cybersecurity/

Center for Security and Assurance in IT (C-SAIT) – Florida State University

- The mission of the Center for Security an Assurance in IT (C-SAIT) is to serve as a focal point for members of different academic disciplines, government, and industry to carry out world-class research and to advance the practice and public awareness of information technology security and assurance through education and public service. The focus of C-SAIT is on innovation and learning.
- http://www.sait.fsu.edu/tour/about.shtml

Center for Cryptology and Information Security – Florida Atlantic University

- "The mission of the Center for Cryptology and Information Security (CCIS) is to promote and advance the state of knowledge, methodology, and training in information security."
- http://math.fau.edu/ccis/

Center for Cybersecurity – University of West Florida

- "Member of the National CyberWatch Center and provides interdisciplinary knowledge crossing Computer Science, Information Technology, Management Information Systems, Electrical Engineering, Criminal Justice, Geospatial Intelligence and Business foundations."
- http://uwf.edu/go/cybersecurity/

Universities

University of South Florida (USF) – Tampa

- Offers a Master of Science in Cybersecurity as well as graduate certificates with concentrations in: Cyber Intelligence; Digital Forensics; Information Assurance; and Computer Security Fundamentals.
- Also offers professional certification training in partnership with $(ISC)^2$
- Will house the state's Center for Cybersecurity
- http://www.usf.edu/innovative-education/programs/online-programs/cybersecurity/masters-degrees.aspx

Florida Institute of Technology (FIT) – Melbourne

- NSA/DHS designated CAE/R
- Offers a Master of Science in Information Assurance and Cybersecurity
- http://www.fit.edu/programs/8098/ms-information-assurance-cybersecurity

University of Central Florida (UCF) – Orlando

- Offers a Master of Science in Digital Forensics
- http://www.ucf.edu/academics/digital-forensics-ms/

Florida State University (FSU) – Tallahassee

- NSA/DHS designated CAE/IAE and CAE/R
- Houses the C-SAIT (see Centers above)
- Has grants for both the NSF Scholarship for Service (SFS) Program and the DoD Information Assurance Scholarship Program (IASP)
- "The courses in Information Security in Computer Science at Florida State University satisfy the National Security Telecommunications and Information Systems Security (NSTISSC) training standard for Information Security Specialists. FSU students that complete the courses specified in the program are uniquely qualified to serve as Information Systems Security (INFOSEC) Professionals."
- http://www.cs.fsu.edu/scholarships/SFS.php

Florida Polytechnic University

- Offers an Information Assurance & Cyber Security concentration in their Computer Science and Information Technology program
- http://floridapolytechnic.org/academics/computer-science-information-technology/information-assurance-cyber-security-2/

Florida Tech (Online University)

- Offers a Master of Science in Information Technology with a Specialization in Cybersecurity
- http://www.floridatechonline.com/programs/graduate-programs/masters-degree/ms-information-technologycybersecurity/

University of West Florida

- Offers interdisciplinary cybersecurity education through two bachelor's degree programs with concentrations in cybersecurity: The BS in Computer Science and the BS in Information Technology: Networking and Communication. Also offers a Master of Science in Administration with a concentration in cybersecurity, as well as certificate programs in: Cybersecurity, Intelligence Analysis, and Information Security Management. Professional certifications in software/technologies are also offered.
- http://uwf.edu/go/cybersecurity/

Valencia

- NSA/DHS designated CAE/2Y
- Offers programs in Digital Forensics, Cybersecurity, Network Security, and Information Assurance
- http://valenciacollege.edu/dfas/

Florida State College at Jacksonville

- NSA/DHS designated CAE/2Y
- Offers numerous IT certifications and concentrations included a Computer Forensics Technician certification
- http://www.fscj.edu/academics/areas-of-study/information-technology

Florida Agricultural and Mechanical University (FAMU)

- NSA/DHS designated CAE/IAE
- Offers NSTISSI 4011 and CNSS 4012 compliant coursework and a certificate program in Information Assurance
- http://www.famu.edu/index.cfm?cis&FCSCIAAboutUs

Nova Southeastern University

- NDA/DHS designated CAE/IAE
- Offers a Master of Science in Information Security (MSIS)
- http://www.scis.nova.edu/masters/msis.html

Florida Atlantic University

- NDA/DHS designated CAE/R
- College of Business offers concentrations/Minors in Information Security and in Risk Management
- http://www.business.fau.edu/undergraduate/minors-certificates/certificates/information-security-certificate/index.aspx

Santa Fe College – Gainesville

- Offers an AS Degree in Networking Systems Technologies with concentrations in Cybersecurity and Digital Forensics. Also offers certifications programs in those concentrations

- http://www.sfcollege.edu/ite/?section=networking

Daytona State College

- Part of the Advanced Cybersecurity Education (ACE) consortium of regional schools developing cybersecurity education
- Offers courses in digital forensics, incident response and network forensics, and Linux administration
- http://www.daytonastate.edu/ace/

Eastern Florida State College

- Offering cybersecurity concentration through AS in Networking Systems Technologies program
- Building a cybersecurity lab on the Palm Bay campus
- http://www.easternflorida.edu/news-events/news-releases/2014/04-21-cyber-security-lab.cfm

Companies

- The (ISC)2 Foundation

Most of the cyber jobs in FL seem to be with government contractors:

- BAE
- TASC
- Lockheed Martin
- Strategic Systems Technology
- SAIC
- Northrop Grumman

Funding

- NSF Scholarship for Service and DoD Information Assurance grants awarded to FSU.

- NSF Advanced Technical Education (ATE) grant awarded to Santa Fe College
- NSF funding is provide for the Advanced Cybersecurity Education (ACE) consortium
- Department of Labor provided funding which allowed Eastern Florida State College to develop a cybersecurity lab

GEORGIA

Georgia currently has 5 NSA-designated CAEs, one of which has also received an NSF Scholarship for Service grant. The big thing in Georgia is the $10 million DHS project investigating open source, being led by Georgia Tech's Research Institute. Also Damballa Labs is located here, a highly respected and well-funded cyber security research company.

State / Policy Activities

There is surprisingly little information on the state level regarding cybersecurity in Georgia. Their state government does not appear to have an office/agency dedicated to security, nor is there a public website providing information on cybersecurity. There is a website for the Georgia Technology Authority, which is the IT-governing agency at the state level, but their website does not have a security focus.

Link: http://gta.georgia.gov/

Centers / Facilities

Damballa Labs

- https://www.damballa.com/
- Moreso a company than a "center," but Damballa does a lot of respected cyber security research. They have also received funding for cyber research from the National Science Foundation, the Department of Homeland Security, the Office of Naval Research, the Air Force Research Labs, the Army Research Office, and Google.

Georgia Tech Information Security Center

- https://www.gtisc.gatech.edu/
- A cross-campus GIT center. Comprised of faculty, staff and students from multiple units across campus, the Georgia Tech Information Security Center (GTISC) is a catalyst for initiating a wide range of activities in both research and education. Members come from the College of Computing, College of Engineering, College of Business, College of Liberal Arts, the Georgia Tech Office of Information Technology (OIT) and the Georgia Tech Research Institute (GTRI).

Center for Information Security Education – Kennesaw State University

- http://infosec.kennesaw.edu/education.html
- Located at Kennesaw State University. The primary purpose of the Center is to provide information on information security educational opportunities and initiatives in the KSU community. The Center also serves to facilitate faculty development in information security and assurance and as the regional host for the Southeast Collegiate Cyber Defense Competition.

Center for Information Security Education - Southern Polytechnic State University

- http://spsu.edu/infosecurity/
- CISE's main goal is to fill the computer security needs for business and educational organizations. The research of the center will revolve around information assurance and security education. The center will bring together researchers with diverse expertise, in partnership with industry, government offices in information assurance and security, local and national institutions to address the complex, interdisciplinary challenges in cyber security and information assurance. The center will integrate research with

education both internally and through a variety of partnership activities. The center will focus on security awareness training and information security education.

Cyber Security Research Institute

- http://www.armstrong.edu/Departments/cyber_security/csec_welcome
- At Armstrong State University. The center is a component of the University Police. The Institute was founded in 2006 as a part of the university's continuing efforts to address the growing cyber security education and training needs of our country's Intelligence, Forensic, Criminal Justice and Law Enforcement professionals. As cyber threats have escalated, the Cyber Security Research Institute is preparing individuals and organizations on the front lines of our defense to investigate, analyze, assure and secure our increasingly vulnerable technology and communications.

Universities

Columbus State University

- CAE/IAE
- https://cs.columbusstate.edu/curriculum/index.php
- The TSYS School of Computer Science offers a large number of undergraduate and graduate degrees, but only two graduate certificate programs seem to focus explicitly on security.

Clark Atlanta University

- CAE/IAE
- http://www.cau.edu/department-of-computer-and-information-science/index.html

- Department of Computer and Information Science offers an MS Degree in Computer Science with optional concentration in Network Security.

Georgia Institute of Technology

- CAE/R
- Offers an MS in Information Security through the School of Computer Science
    - http://www.scs.gatech.edu/future/msinfosec
- Offers a professional education cybersecurity certificate program
    - http://www.pe.gatech.edu/cyber-security/cyber-security-certificate
- Has the multi-disciplinary Information Security Center that focuses on research and education.

Kennesaw State University

- CAE/IAE
- http://infosec.kennesaw.edu/education.html
- Coordinated through the Center for Information Security Education, the University offers a number of degrees and concentrations including: A Bachelor of Business Administration in Information Security and Assurance, a minor in Information Security and Assurance, and undergraduate and graduate certificates in Information Security, and Criminal Justice Degrees examining Technology and CyberCrime.
- Also hosts the Southeast Collegiate Cyber Defense Competition (SECCDC)
    - http://www.seccdc.org/

- Bachelor of Business Administration in Information Security and Assurance was named as a finalist for Best Cyber Higher Education Program by SC Magazine in 2013.
    - http://awards.scmagazine.com/best-cyber-higher-education-program-0

Southern Polytechnic State University

- CAE/IAE
- http://spsu.edu/infosecurity/degree_programs/index.htm
- Offers undergraduate and graduate programs in Information Technology with specializations in Information Security and Assurance. Also offers a graduate-level certificate in Information Security an Assurance.

Armstrong State University

- Offers a graduate certificate in Cyber Crime.
    - http://armstrong.edu/Majors/degree/cyber_affairs_cyber_security
- The College of Science & Technology offers undergraduate and graduate degrees in Computer Science and Information Technology.
    - http://www.armstrong.edu/index.php/Science_and_Technology/cst_welcome
- Has the Cyber Security Research Institute.

Companies

- Damballa Labs
- GlobalCrypto
- Gyrus
- Lancope
- Purewire

- Whisper Communications
- Dell
- ICF International
- NSSPlus
- SRA International, Inc.
- Indrasoft
- Information Innovators, Inc.
- Siemens Industry, Inc.
- PwC
- North American Electric Reliability Corporation (NERC)
- Network Security Systems Plus
- Solutions By Design II, LLC
- CoSolutions, Inc.
- Next Generation
- TAD PGS, Inc.
- Lockheed Martin
- Noblis
- Apple & Associates Inc.

Funding

The U.S. Department of Homeland Security (DHS) Science and Technology (S&T) Directorate has named the Georgia Tech Research Institute (GTRI) to lead implementation efforts for the five-year, $10 million Homeland Open Security Technology (HOST) program. The HOST program will investigate open source and open cyber security methods, models and technologies, and identify viable and sustainable approaches that support national cyber security objectives.

- http://gtri.gatech.edu/casestudy/gtri-lead-10-million-department-homeland-security-

HAWAII

Only one Hawaii college is designated as an NSA center of academic excellence: Honolulu Community College. A new "Cyber Range" at UH Manoa collaborates with DoD and focuses on cyber warfare training exercises and infrastructure protection. The current governor has been working towards strengthening Hawaii's cybersecurity focus.

State / Policy Activities

The Hawaiian governor recently appointed a Chief adviser for Technology and Cybersecurity in a move to tighten ties with the federal government and build Hawaii's cybersecurity profile. Recent legislature and state government organizations focus on cyber crime, cyber bullying/stalking and exploitation of children. Government organizations include: The Hawaii Internet & Technology Crimes (HITeC) Unit and The Hawaii Internet Crimes Against Children (HICAC) Task Force.

Recent Hawaii state laws focusing on cyber-related issues: (taken from: http://www.hawaiireporter.com/groundbreaking-cyber-crime-bills-become-law/123)

- **HB 1777**: authorizes judges in Hawaii's State court system to require that certain records located or held by entities outside Hawaii be released to the prosecution or defense in a criminal case. Prosecutors will now be able to obtain evidence that is often in the hands of mainland corporations, such as cell phone records.

- **HB 1788**: a cybercrime omnibus bill, strengthens existing computer crime laws by making computer fraud laws mirror Hawaii's identify theft laws; the result is that accessing a computer with the intent to commit theft becomes a more serious offense. The law also imposes harsher penalties by reclassifying the severity of computer fraud and unauthorized computer access offenses. Notably, the bill creates the new offense of Computer Fraud in the Third Degree, a class C felony; this particular crime would involve knowingly accessing a computer, computer system, or computer network with intent to commit theft in the third or fourth degree.

- **HB 2295**: expands the existing offense of Use of a Computer in the Commission of a Separate Crime to include situations where a perpetrator knowingly uses a computer to pursue, conduct surveillance on, contact, harass, annoy, or alarm the victim or intended victim of the crimes of Harassment under HRS 711-1106 or Harassment by Stalking under HRS 711 1106.5. This law recognizes that using a computer to commit such crimes is an aggravating factor that justifies an additional penalty.

- **SB 2222**: addresses "sexting." The bill would create two new offenses in HRS chapter 712 that would: Prohibit an adult from intentionally or knowingly soliciting a minor to electronically transmit a nude image (photo or video) of a minor to any person (misdemeanor); prohibit a minor from knowingly electronically transmitting a nude image of him/herself or any other minor to any person, or intentionally or knowingly soliciting another minor to do so (petty misdemeanor); and prohibit a person of any age from knowingly possessing a nude image transmitted by a minor (but a person charged with this crime would have an affirmative defense that he/she made reasonable efforts to destroy the nude image (petty misdemeanor).

Centers / Facilities

Cyber Range - UH Mānoa campus

- http://www.kaleo.org/news/new-cyber-range-promotes-cyber-security/article_fea371f2-fd7b-11e2-8312-0019bb30f31a.html root9B Cybersecurity Research, Training and Operations facility – Honolulu

- http://premieralliance.com/latest-news/root9b-establishes-cutting%E2%80%90edge-cybersecurity-facility-in-hawaii

Referentia Systems' Cyber Collaboration Center (CCC) – Honolulu

- http://www.referentia.com/cyber-collaboration-center

Pacific Center for Advanced Technology Training (PCATT)

- http://pcatt.org/
- A not-for-profit consortium of the University of Hawai'i Community Colleges. The mission of PCATT is to provide leadership and training in advanced technologies to enhance economic and workforce development programs and initiatives in the State of Hawai'i and the Pacific Rim.
- Security Courses: http://pcatt.org/index.php/category/security

Universities

The University of Hawaii system

- http://www.hawaii.edu/
- Various courses offered in cybersecurity at different campuses
- Cyber Range at UH Manoa hosts cyber competitions and collaborates with DoD/military

Honolulu Community College

- National Center of Academic Excellence in Information Assurance Education Two-Year (CAE2Y)

- Cybersecurity Center: http://www2.honolulu.hawaii.edu/?q=node/823
- Academic Credit Programs
    o The core Information Assurance program at Honolulu CC is the Computing Electronics & Networking Technology (CENT) Program. The CENT program provides students with a wide background in Information and Communication Technology. Imbedded in this program is a Certificate of Achievement (CA) in Information Assurance (IA). The CA in IA is built on the knowledge unit requirements for a collegiate institution to be recognized as a CAE2Y. The program also features support for the following industry recognized certifications: A+, LINUX +, Security +, CCNA, and MCP. In addition, the CENT program also offers a third year of study which articulates to the Bachelors of Applied Science in Information Security Assurance at the University of Hawaii at West Oahu.
- Non Credit Programs
    o The non-credit continuing education course offerings at Honolulu CC, is supported by the Pacific Center for Advanced Technology Training (PCATT). PCATT offers an extensive selection of Cybersecurity related courses for industry professionals looking to upgrade their skills or learn new skills. Cybersecurity related courses offered include, Security +, CISSP, CEH, CCNA Security, MCSE and much more. PCATT also offers customized training to meet the needs of your organization.

Chaminade University

- Private university that offers cybersecurity education through their computer science program

- http://www.chaminade.edu/computer-science/
- Offers a "Networks and Security" degree concentration

Companies

- Referentia Systems
- root9B
- Booz Allen

Funding

The University of Hawaii – West Oʻahu received a $245,000 grant from the Office of Naval Research to establish a Science Technology Engineering Math (STEM) Center of Excellence at the University.

Other Notations

Sanjeev "Sonny" Bhagowalia, chief advisor for technology and cybersecurity, earned the 2014 Government Technology Research Alliance (GTRA) "Government Innovator of the Year" award. Bhagowalia received the award for facilitating Hawaii's business and technology transformation, launched in 2011 under the Abercrombie Administration.

- http://governor.hawaii.gov/blog/governors-chief-advisor-for-technology-and-cybersecurity-wins-national-government-innovator-of-the-year-award/

IDAHO

While Idaho is not a highly populated state, it does have quality IA education and research. Idaho currently has 2 NSA-designated CAEs, both of which have received NSF Scholarship for Service grants. Idaho State University has a well-established and long-running SFS program. Idaho State University is also a founding and sponsoring member of the Colloquium for Information Systems Security Education (cisse.info).

In addition to IA university programs, Idaho National Labs is the DoE's lead nuclear research and development facility, and ICS-CERT has a location in Idaho Falls as well. This provides a collaborative environment between students and faculty at the universities and leading research and response efforts from the public and private sectors through INL and ICS-CERT.

State / Policy Activities

Idaho state government has a cybersecurity awareness website that provides useful links and information for home users, tens, kids, businesses, and educators. This site also links to state agencies dealing with cybersecurity including their Incident Response process, the Idaho Office of the CIO Security Services, and the state government policies, standards, and guidelines. It is a well-done website with a lot of information that goes beyond the cyber-related sites put up by many other state governments.

- http://cybersecurity.idaho.gov/

Recently, the Idaho Department of Finance began taking part in a national project to better understand the cybersecurity practices of state-registered investment advisers, which make up more than half of the registered investment advisers conducting business in the United States.

- http://www.govtech.com/state/Idaho-Takes-Part-in-Investment-Adviser-Cybersecurity-Project-.html

Centers / Facilities

Center for Secure and Dependable Systems (CSDS)

- http://www.uidaho.edu/engr/csds
- At the University of Idaho. Completely self-funded, the center brings together collaborative research efforts and serves as an educational focal point for the design, development, analysis, and use of technologies that result in secure and dependable computing systems. CSDS is one of the centers in the College of Engineering at the University of Idaho.

National Information Assurance Training and Education Center (NIATEC)

- http://niatec.info/ViewPage.aspx?id=0
- Associated with Idaho State University Center of Academic Excellence, NIATEC is a consortium of academic, industry, and government organizations to improve the literacy, awareness, training and education standards in Information Assurance.

Universities

Idaho State University

- CAE/IAE
- http://security.isu.edu/ViewPage.aspx?id=252
- Perhaps unsurprisingly, this school's program seems quite similar to the University of Washington's. From their website: "The security program at Idaho State University is a comprehensive interdisciplinary program that is characterized by joint student and faculty involvement in learning and research. Everyone in expected to participate in an active, intentional learning process. Learning is continuous. There is a constant interchange of

information in both formal and informal classes and learning events. There are frequent seminars and classes offered during the week; these are led by both students and faculty. Students design their own learning projects that lead to research papers and thesis opportunities."

University of Idaho

- CAE/IAE
- http://www.uidaho.edu/engr/csds/academics
- The Center for Secure and Dependable Systems offers a Computer Science-based Information Assurance curriculum through undergraduate and graduate-level degrees—including a PhD in CS with IA focus.

Companies

- Idaho National Laboratory
- Bernett Research
- CradlePoint
- McAfee
- TEKsystems
- TEG GLOBAL
- POWER Engineers, Inc.
- Synoptek
- Sinclair Broadcast Group
- CH2M HILL
- Virtual IT, Inc.
- Micron Technology, Inc.
- CenturyLink
- NHR Global
- Leidos

Funding

- NSF Scholarship for Service grants awarded to University of Idaho and Idaho State University.

ILLINOIS

Illinois has a healthy economy in the cybersecurity arena and 8 CAE institutions. There are a plethora of positions advertised in the areas of digital forensics, policy and risk management. Argonne National Labs and the University of Illinois – Urbana being engaged with internet development in the late 1960s, coupled with metropolitan Chicago being a Midwest hub of commerce – cybersecurity is thriving in the scientific and corporate worlds.

In 2010 Illinois received a $1million grant to develop cybersecurity first responded training to be rolled out nationally, the state has a fair amount of sophistication and positions itself as a leader in cybersecurity curriculum development and positioning the state / economy as a leader in the field.

State / Policy Activities

The governor's office is taking a proactive approach to linking state policy with the development of cyber awareness and building awareness of cybersecurity career fields through well-spaced public relations announcements, attracting veterans into the career field and free on-line competitions through cyber aces and Illinois' CAE2Y. The state proudly displays their involvement in the MSIAS.

Illinois has had a cyber crimes / internet crimes unit since 2007. The State of Illinois has an emphasis on cyber crime – driven by the Illinois Computer Crime Institute, in the office of the Attorney General's Hi-Tech Crimes Bureau. The state has diversified their interest in cyber security – among crime, energy, defense, with an emphasis on legislation regarding cyber bulling and government regulation of cyber stalking.

Centers / Facilities

Argonne National Labs provides a mature setting for Network and Cybersecurity research, commercialization opportunities. The Lab provides internships and promotes a stable research facility promoting cybersecurity research, educational and entrepreneurial opportunities. Argonne maintains four laboratory sites within Illinois, Lemont, Carbondale, Chicago and Champlaign, Network Labs Chicago has served as the host city for the CIO Executive Summit coordinated by Evanta. Illinois's plethora of corporations serves as a magnet for a conference attracting CIO leaders from major companies. Evanta hosts senior leadership conferences in 27 major US cities. Cyber security team wins 2009 DOE innovation, technology achievement award.

Information Trust Institute, at UI-Champaign-Urbana, is a mature research institution with well-defined research pathways. While part of the UI. Champaign-Urbana, the ITI just celebrated its 10 year anniversary. The organization focuses internally and externally, working with Department of Energy, the NSA and receives grant money from a wide variety of other funders. The ITI is a model to be considered.

Universities

Illinois has eight Academic Centers of Excellence; six of the eight (De Paul University, Illinois Institute of Technology, Illinois State University, Lewis University and Southern Illinois University are dedicated to Information Assurance, one is a two year school< Moraine Valle Community College. The University of Illinois at Urbana Champaign is a CAE/IAE, CAE/R.

DePaul University

DePaul University offers a BS in Information Assurance and Security Engineering students will learn the fundamentals of information security, security infrastructure design and implementation, computer forensics, risk assessment as well as the impact of security requirements on a business operation. Students learn to design, implement, integrate and manage various security infrastructure components through hands-on activities in our state-of the-art Information Assurance and Security Laboratory. There is also an MS in Computer, Information and Network Security intended for students who wish to specialize in the security aspects of the Information Technology field.

Illinois Institute of Technology

Illinois Institute of Technology, School of Applied Technology, focuses on the intersection of cyber security and forensics providing a targeted holistic approach through the Center for Cyber Security and Forensics Education C2SAFE.

Illinois State University through the Center for Information Assurance and Cybersecurity Education wants to lead Illinois, and nationwide. "to provide premier undergraduate and distinguished graduate programs for the education of computing and telecommunications professionals, to support other academic units.

Lewis University

Lewis University offers a range of undergraduate a graduate certificates in both information Assurance and cybersecurity, as well as more technical degrees around network security.

Moraine Valley Community College

Moraine Valley Community College – a CAE/2Y is also one of the two locations of the cyber aces http://www.cyberaces.org/academies an innovative approach to accelerating on-line education and training into the cybersecurity workforce in the areas of Advanced Forensics, Penetration Testing, Hardware, Industrial Control Systems, Perimeter Defense.

University of Illinois

University of Illinois has two campuses with separate CAE/IAE designations, UI Springfield and UI-Urbana Champaign. The latter campus holds a CAE/R classification. UI Springfield participates in the SFS scholarship program and maintains a team of cyberaces. The University has received $50,000 support from State Farms to build a lab to support cybersecurity. Earlier in 2014 the University hosted the Cyber Defense and Disaster Recovery Conference 2014. UI / Champaign - Urbana cybersecurity unit is the Information Trust Institute (ITI). This award winning organization has five research areas: data science, evaluation, health information, power grid, and systems and networking. ITI has sponsored its 10th annual cyber related conference. This school presents as a mature CAE/R supporting a strong institute, the ITI, connecting to five different areas of the economy.

Southern Illinois University

Southern Illinois University – Carbondale, is a CAE/IAE has a technically oriented program. And they now have Sam Chung.

Companies

Illinois has a healthy economy for cybersecurity. Listings of companies in cybersecurity include:

- BAE Systems Applied Intelligence
- Boeing
- Booz Allen Hamilton
- BRIDGE Energy Group
- Collabera
- Collegis Education
- CoreLogix Consulting Inc.
- Crowe Horwath LLP
- Deloitte
- Encode Inc.
- Fiberlink
- IBM
- KPMG
- Lockheed Martin
- ManTech International Corporation
- Navigant Consulting
- Netra Technologies, Inc.
- Northern Trust Corporation
- Northrop Grumman
- Olenick & Associates

- Ordusion Technologies, Inc.
- PwC
- Stroz Friedberg
- Verizon
- West Monroe Partners
- Wilson Elser

Illinois has a healthy economy for cybersecurity. Listings of companies with cyberecurity needs in Illinois include:

- Lockheed Martin
- Navigant Consulting
- CoreLogix Consulting Inc.
- BRIDGE Energy Group
- Netra Technologies, Inc.
- Encode Inc.
- PwC
- BAE Systems Applied Intelligence
- Ordusion Technologies, Inc.
- West Monroe Partners
- Crowe Horwath LLP
- Northrop Grumman
- ManTech International Corporation
- Collabera
- Collegis Education
- Verizon
- Boeing
- All State
- Walgreen's
- Kraft
- Catapillar
- Johnson Controls
- Sourcefire

Other Notations

1) http://www.ides.illinois.gov/Lists/News%20and%20Announcements/DispForm.aspx?ID=31

2) http://www.cyberaces.org/academies

3) http://thenextweb.com/insider/2013/03/29/illinois-looks-to-boost-its-tech-prowess-with-new-governor-led-cybersecurity-competition-for-vets/

4) http://www.illinois.gov/ready/Pages/default.aspx

5) https://msisac.cisecurity.org/members/state-government/

INDIANA

Indiana, while not the earliest adopter of an integrated cybersecurity approach, is ahead of the pack in pulling together a multi-pronged approach to addressing economic, military and educational issues. Starting in 2005, through the leadership of Purdue University, there has been a cybersecurity presence in the state.

State / Policy Activities

Indiana has well defined cybersecurity laws and policy. The Universities drive cyber activities within the state, as does the government sector. There was an October Cybersecurity Forum, October 2014, supported by DHS.

Centers / Facilities

Indiana University umbrellas a variety of 'centers' described below. These departments have worked closely together for the past 11 years under the leadership of Fred Cates.

Indiana Cyber Security Center (ICSC), established 2005, has been based in Purdue and collaborates with military, fiscal/economic and educational clusters across the state.

The Indiana University Center for Applied Cybersecurity Research has named Von Welch director. He has been the center's deputy director since 2011 and has been working with the ICSC since before 2005.

Mauer School of Law at Indiana University/Bloomington serves as a resource for national, foreign and international cybersecurity law.

IN Cyber is a K-12 Charter School that promotes quality cybersecurity, technical education. IN Cyber promotes intellectual and personal development through professionally focused and formative learning opportunities, While the school has doubled its enrollment in two years, the institution faces a law suit for non-payment of $600,000 to National Network of Digital Schools

Universities

Indiana has three NIETP centers of Academic Excellence. Ivy is the CAE 2Y; Purdue University is and Indiana State University holds all three designations, as a CAE, CAE-R, IA.

Companies

- Boeing
- CDI Corporation
- Crowe Horwath
- Duke Energy Systems
- Exelis
- First Financial Corporation
- GHR Global
- IBM
- Kingfisher Systems
- Knowledge Consulting
- NiSource
- PwC
- Volt Workforce Solutions

Other Notations

1) http://www.in.gov/iot/files/Information_Security_Framework.pdf

2) http://csrc.nist.gov/nice/2013workshop/presentations/day1/d1_trk4_dark_vargas_indiana_cybersecurity_service_center.pdf

3) http://www.go2incyber.org/

4) http://www.idsnews.com/article/2013/02/students-easily-find-jobs-in-cyber-security-field

5) https://protect.iu.edu/cybersecurity/data/laws/IN

6) https://www.insideindianabusiness.com/newsitem.asp?ID=65900

7) http://www.indy.gov/eGov/City/DPS/DHS/Pages/Cyber-Security-Awareness.aspx

IOWA

Iowa has a relatively high level of cybersecurity activity. The state does not have the size or perhaps the breadth of other larger more well-funded states but it excels in a number of key areas. The state has a normal posture regarding cybersecurity laws and government activity. The education system offering IA learning and research is small but very active. Particularly Iowa State University is a recognized thought leader and a Center of Academic Excellence. The state lacks major cyber research centers but is relatively well funded in areas like smart grid security. Private sector tech companies are not as numerous as in other coastal states but the research parks attached to ISU and Iowa University show a respectable smattering of private sector tech entities. In conclusion, Iowa is graded solidly as a medium strength cyber state that very definitely "punches above its weight."

State / Policy Activities

Iowa became the 43rd state to enact data breach notifications laws with CHAPTER 715C PERSONAL INFORMATION SECURITY BREACH PROTECTION. Recently, the state amended the law to require notice be provided to the Iowa attorney general. April 8 -- *Iowa Gov. Terry Branstad (R) recently signed legislation (S.F. 2259) that amends the state's data breach notification law to require covered entities to notify the state attorney general of breaches affecting more than 500 Iowans.*

http://www.bna.com/iowa-enacts-breach-n17179889559/

Centers / Facilities

At Iowa State University there is a research park with a large tenant list of technology companies -- http://www.isupark.org/. There is also a research park at the neighboring Iowa University.

Universities

One NSA CAE located at Iowa State University (ISU). Their SFS program is ran out of the school's Information Assurance Center -- http://www.iac.iastate.edu/. Also at ISU, there is the Power Infrastructure Cybersecurity Laboratory

http://powercyber.ece.iastate.edu/.

The lab is described as... *The electric power grid is a highly automated network that uses a variety of sensors, information and control systems, and communication networks for the purpose of monitoring, protection and control of the grid. The recent findings, as documented in federal reports and in the literature, indicate the growing threat of cyber-based attacks in numbers and sophistication on the nation's electric grid and other critical infrastructure systems. Therefore, cyber security of the power grid — encompassing attack prevention, detection, mitigation, and resilience — is among the most important research issues of today and in the future.*

Additionally, ISU was working on one of the earliest university and corporate collaborations funded by the NSF... *The new Center for Information Protection, funded mostly through membership fees paid by cybersecurity vendors and users, will focus on short-term cybersecurity issues, possibly including research on methods to comply with federal regulations such as Sarbanes-Oxley, said Doug Jacobson, an Iowa State engineering professor and CTO at Palisade Systems, a network management and security vendor*

http://www.networkworld.com/article/2314287/lan-wan/nsf--iowa-state-to-launch-cybersecurity-center.html.

Western Iowa Tech University provides a cybersecurity curriculum. University of Northern Iowa has a cybersecurity focused computer science program. Southeastern Community College offers a network security and cybersecurity AAS diploma.

Companies

For a list of many technology companies operating in Iowa check the tenant list for the ISU research park

http://www.isupark.org/tenants/directory/.

KANSAS

Cyber Security Legislation

The state legislation (Chapter 50, Article 7a) specifically addresses issue of Information Security (Cybersecurity) which includes protection of consumer information.

Research Centers and Collaborations

To help counter the threat, the National Science Foundation has awarded $2.3 million to Kansas State University's department of computing and information sciences to provide scholarships to qualified students interested in becoming cybersecurity and information assurance professionals. A newly developed course by the computing and information sciences department, Cyber Defense Basics, uses a contained off-the-grid cybersecurity lab for mock exercises. The lab allows instructors to test students' abilities to defend against cyber attacks without infecting systems outside the lab. It teaches students the basics of cyber defense and how to counterattack.

Research Partners

Kansas State University faculty is involved in a variety of domestic and international collaborations with academic, industry, and federal agencies in the area of information assurance. These collaborations include, but are not limited to industry partners such as Microsoft Research, Cerner, Telcordia, Rockwell-Collins, and HP Labs; federal agencies such as the Idaho National Lab (DOE), the U.S. Army Command and General Staff College, the US Army Computer networking and Electronic Warfare Proponent, the US National Institute for Standards and Technology; international collaborations such as Defense Research and Development Canada; and academic institutions such as Princeton, Purdue, Penn State, Stevens Institute, and Georgia Tech. Other collaborators include:

Corporate

- Microsoft Research
- Cerner
- Telcordia
- Rockwell-Collins
- HP Labs

Governmental

- Idaho National Laboratory
- US Army Command and General Staff College
- US Army Computer Network Operations and Electronic Warfare Proponent
- National Institute for Standards and Technology
- Department of Homeland Security
- National Security Agency
- Defense Research and Development Canada

Academic

- Princeton University
- Purdue University
- Pennsylvania State University
- Stevens Institute of Technology
- Georgia Institute of Technology

Research Focus

Cyber Defense, Cybersecurity labs, Cybersecurity, Information Assurance, Analytic Forensics, Android Security, Anthropology & Security, Cloud Security, Moving-target Defense and Secure Real-time OS

Facilities

One major facility is the Argus Lab located at Kansas State University. Argus research has been supported by the National Science Foundation, Department of Defense, Department of Energy, National Institute of Standards and Technology, and HP Labs. The group is named after the giant Argus in Greek mythology, who has a hundred eyes that constantly watch for enemies. The Argus group was founded by Dr. Xinming (Simon) Ou in 2006 to carry out cyber security research. Our focus is on the defense aspect of the cyber space, and our philosophy is to start from real problems, and create solutions that last. Our research attempts to address the root causes of the various cybersecurity problems, and we work closely with industry to ensure our work both addresses the most pressing problems of the time, and provides the scientific basis for solutions that can stand the test of time.

Funding Opportunities and Source(s)

Research Funding through Kansas State University:

1) Automatic Control-Network Security Management Using Attack Graphs. Department of Energy. $35K, 3/20/2007 - 8/17/2007.

2) CT-ISG: Model-Based, Automatic Network Security Management. National Science Foundation. $245K, 8/1/2007 -7/31/2009.

3) REU:CT-ISG: Model-Based, Automatic Network Security Management. National Science Foundation. $6K, 8/1/2007 - 7/31/2009.

4) National Science Foundation has awarded $2.3 towards training and research

5) Support for start-ups

6) No available information found

References

1) http://gohsep.la.gov/cybersecurity.aspx

2) http://csc.latech.edu/

3) http://www.dhs.gov/science-and-technology-directorate-cyber-security-division

4) http://www.kslegislature.org/li/

5) http://www.legis.la.gov/legis/home.aspx

6) http://www.leg.state.or.us/

7) http://www.oregon.gov/DAS/CIO/ISRC/pages/index.aspx

8) http://techoregon.org/cyber-studies-strategy-oregon

9) https://www.osbar.org/publications/bulletin/14febmar/nsa.html

10) http://www.pdx.edu/computer-science/

11) https://msisac.cisecurity.org/about/workgroups/legis-resources.cfm

12) http://www.cisa.ksu.edu/research-systems-security.php

13) http://www.nsf.gov/cise/funding/cyber_awards.jsp

14) http://www.arguslab.org/

15) http://www.k-state.edu/media/newsreleases/jun13/cybercorps91313.html

KENTUCY

Kentucky is a latecomer to the field in cybersecurity, and, sounding very similar to South Carolina as one of the poster-child states of 'what not to do' in cybersecurity. In 2012, the state finance cabinet posted social security numbers on their website.[1] A bright spot in Kentucky is the job market, possibly because Kentucky businesses are trying to come up to speed with the rest of the pack.

State / Policy Activities

This year, Kentucky passed two bills which now require local government agencies notify people within 35 days of PII being mishandled or stolen.

Kentucky is the 47th state in the union to pass cybersecurity laws. House Bill 232, went into effect in July and outlined the reporting requirements if a security breach occurs. House Bill 5 is a data privacy bill that imposes data-security requirements, investigation requirements and breach notification requirements on governmental agencies and "nonaffiliated third parties" that do business with governmental agencies.[2]

The state's cyberbullying laws are covered under Kentucky's bullying legislation and are mentioned specifically as being under the purview of the Kentucky's educational system.

Centers / Facilities

City of Lexington partnered with DHS to offer a Kentucky Cybersecurity Summit in October, 2014.

---

[1] http://www.courier-journal.com/story/news/politics/ky-legislature/2014/03/21/cyber-security-bill-clears-kentucky-senate/6711011/ The Courier=Journal March, 2014 story on cybersecurity legislation.

[2] http://www.bizjournals.com/louisville/news/2014/08/11/what-are-the-repercussions-for-not-following-cyber.html?page=all

Universities

Kentucky is one of 7 states without a CAE institution. Kentucky State University is offering a cybersecurity option within the Division of Computer Science. Northern Kentucky University College of Informatics is stepping up their cyber security program and took 3rd in the 2014 Southeast Collegiate Cyber Defense Competition (SECCDC). NKU is offering an 18 hour on-line basic cybersecurity certificate.

Companies

- Wyatt Tarrant & Combs LLP's
- Kindred Health Care
- SIAC
- Time Warner Cable
- Kentucky Lottery Corporation
- PerspecSys, Inc
- Ebit
- West Corporation
- Anchor Point Technology Resources
- CyberCoders
- Calance US
- Kforce
- RehabCare Group
- Analysts International Corporation
- Louisville Metro Government
- Request Technology
- LG&E and KU Energy

Other Notations

- http://insiderlouisville.com/opinion/kentuckys-new-cyber-security-statutes-will-change-business/

LOUISIANA

Cyber Security Legislation

Legislation Act 772 – 2001 regulates all Information Technology related policies. This includes IT Governance, Security Policies, Computer Infrastructure and General Policies. This has been revised with few additions (La. Rev. Stat. § 51:3071 et seq. (Acts 2005, No. 499, §1, eff. Jan. 1, 2006.))

Research Centres and Collaborations

The Center for Secure Cyberspace (CSC) is a joint collaboration between Louisiana Tech University and Louisiana State University created to assist faculty members in their research, and to support federal, state, and private sector cyberspace security needs in collaboration with the Cyber Innovation Center (CIC) in Bossier City, Louisiana. The CSC also capitalizes upon world-class resources of the Louisiana Optical Network Initiative and Louisiana Tech's Institution for Micromanufacturing.

Louisiana is home to a number of cyber related centers of expertise. An example is the Cyber Innovation Center adjacent to Barksdale AFB. This center is owned by the State of Louisiana and built to support the cyber defense efforts of the United States 8th Air Force. This facility is capable of development work at classified and unclassified levels. SDMI has also begun to associate a national university coalition. On March 27, 2013, it was announced that IBM was locating a software development and engineering office to employ 800 persons in Baton Rouge. Part of the attraction to IBM was partnering with the LSU School of Computer Science and Engineering. LSU is building a world class program and will soon offer a Master's of Science in Cyber Security.

Louisiana State Police Training Academy also organizes training for law enforcement officers, investigators and supervisors strategies and tactics for investigating cyber-related (online) crimes and best practices for providing cyber security

Research Focus

The Core Research Team and their students have collaboratively worked on rare and event pattern detection, malware and botnets, anomaly detection, cyber forensics, information fusion, secure information dissemination, grid computation, interactive visualization, adversarial cyber-behavioral biometrics, unmanned aerial vehicles and sensor networks. Other critical areas are Critical Infrastructure Protection, Intrusion Prevention and Threat Assessment.

Cyber Security Facilities

The Cyberspace Research Laboratory at Louisiana Tech is a state of the art facility for cyber centric experimentation. It has advanced virtualization, visualization as well as network capabilities. It also includes a micro aerial vehicle and wireless sensor network laboratory and an FPGA laboratory. In order to visualize complex data, our visualization system gives researchers the ability to render large datasets and run graphical simulations on a high-resolution tiled display. As for network capabilities, the advanced networking lab offers a variety of Cisco equipment for testing different types of networks.

Funding Opportunities and Source(s)

No relevant information on this subject.

MAINE

Maine does not have a generally high level of cybersecurity activity but there are a few areas of interest to us that deserve merit and attention. Firstly, the state has the requisite data breach laws and a relatively active state government offering information and participating in some conferences targeting IA/CD. The research and education capacity of the state is rather small. The number of degree options -- especially at the baccalaureate or graduate level -- are very minimal but there are some interesting facilities gaining ground. For example, the Maine Cybersecurity Cluster at the Univ. of Southern Maine is a relatively unique albeit quite nascent attempt at providing students and researchers with a virtual attack and defense environment. In general, the level of activity is low but there is a groundswell of effort and the development of the USM cluster should likely be further investigated after it gains some maturity.

State / Policy Activities

Maine has a standard boiler plate data breach notification law

http://www.mainelegislature.org/legis/statutes/10/title10sec1348.html.

The state offers a portal with useful information on identity theft, privacy rights, and cybersecurity relevant information. The state's governor has called for and praised the efforts of cybersecurity practitioners and researchers in the state. The state has also hosted government conferences on topics like security and big data. The state has also exercised with their National Guard units and universities to boost their cybersecurity readiness.

Centers / Facilities

Recently, the University of Southern Maine has setup the Maine Cybersecurity Cluster -- http://mcsc.usm.maine.edu/. The Cluster aims to provide student training, conduct assessments, perform lab studies, and provide a space for research and development in cybersecurity. The Cluster is described as...*USM came up with the idea to create a cybersecurity lab about* four years ago. Using $1 million in grants from the National Science Foundation and Maine Technology Institute, educators were able to design and build the lab. Part of the grant money also went toward building a private network, which will allow students to work with computer viruses without the threat of it spreading to other networks. Students will also examine technical, legal and ethical issues surrounding the collection, sharing and theft of sensitive data.

http://www.wcsh6.com/story/news/local/2014/08/26/cybersecurity-lab-usm-data-theft/14607533/

University of Maine has a homeland security lab that focuses on information security. The lab is described as... *The University of Maine Homeland Security Lab is an inter-disciplinary group that works closely with groups having an interest in developing homeland security. The University of Maine Homeland Security Lab is dedicated to carrying out research that can help anticipate and protect against terrorist attacks and other disasters. It is also interested in the problems of the first responder.*

http://homeland.maine.edu/

Universities

There are no NSA Centers of Academic Excellence in Maine and really there are relatively scant options for budding cybersecurity students looking to study in Maine.

In addition to their cybersecurity cluster, the University of Southern Maine is also hoping to soon offer a specific cybersecurity degree program. University of Maine does not offer specific cybersecurity degrees but does offer courses and research opportunities through their college of informatics. University of Maine – Fort Kent is currently the only UM system affiliate to offer a specific cybersecurity degree option. They are also part of the virtual lab project mentioned earlier. They will use the lab as an integral part of the training of new cybersecurity students. At the two-year level there is interest in cybersecurity. For example, York County Community College is tied in with the above mentioned Maine Cybersecurity Cluster.

MARYLAND

- The vision is to become the epicenter for cyber. And it looks like they are making very good progress.
- They have tons of state backing. Example state activities include:
    - Implementation of a cyber investment tax credit for companies as an incentive.
    - Implementation of an InvestMaryland Program Initiative for growth companies.
    - Creation of a Commission on Cybersecurity Innovation and Excellence.
    - Creation of a Resource Center for Cybersecurity (co-led by Maryland and Michigan).
    - Creation of a Baltimore/Washington task force to implement a strategy for cyber around CYBERCOM activities.
    - Creation of a Director of Cyber Development.
- They have several incubators/innovation centers.
- From 2008 to 2012, they had 374 VC deals valued at $2,096,999.00
- Five four-year colleges and universities in Greater Baltimore have been recognized by the NSA as excellent institutions for education and research in information assurance.
- There are over 75,000 employed in Cyber Security-related jobs in the Greater Baltimore/Central Maryland region. In addition, there are nearly 20,000 open Cyber Security job positions in Maryland.
- There are currently more than 11,000 companies in Maryland that create products and services to protect against cyber attacks,

including heavy hitters such as Northrop Grumman, JHU APL, Verizon, Lockheed, Booz Allen, SAIC, and CSC.

State / Policy Activities

In May, the Governor signed a new Cybersecurity Investment Incentive Tax Credit. Funded at $3M, the Cybersecurity Investment Incentive Tax Credit provides a refundable tax credit (beginning 2014) to qualified Maryland cybersecurity companies that seek and secure capital from an in-state or out-of-state investor. The tax credit also specifically encourages out-of-state investors to contribute to Maryland cybersecurity companies.[1] Stipulations include:

- The credit is first come-first served,
- Investor must invest at least $25,000,
- Must apply to Maryland Department of Business and Economic Development for certification,
- Company must be based in Maryland and in business for no longer than five years,
- Total capitalization of at least $100,000,
- Owns or licenses proprietary technology,
- Fewer than 50 employees,
- Ownership interest is not publicly traded.

The Governor also has an **InvestMaryland Program Initiative**. It is a funding source for early, mid and late state growth companies. Since 2012, select Maryland companies and venture capital firms have benefitted from the program, funded by $84 million raised by the state's first online auction of premium insurance tax credits. InvestMaryland funds are apportioned through the following three programs

---

[1] http://mgaleg.maryland.gov/webmga/frmMain.aspx?pid=billpage&tab=subject3&stab=01&id=hb0803&ys=2013RS

- Venture capital firms
- Maryland Venture Fund
- Equity participation investment program

TEDCO

Fund invests in start-up cyber security technologies for Maryland based companies with more than 16 full-time employees and less than $500,000 in outside investments. Investments per company will not exceed $100,000.

Maryland Commission on Cybersecurity Innovation and Excellence

State Delegate Susan Lee, who was instrumental in creating and served as co-chair of the Identity Theft Task Force, spearheaded the creation of the Maryland Commission on Cybersecurity Innovation and Excellence. The commission's mission is to review the state's cyber laws and policies and to develop strategies that protect against future cyber attacks, while also helping spur cybersecurity innovation and job creation.

The Commission's responsibility

- Legal Strategy
- State Structure & Best Practices Model
- Training and Education Plan
- Marketing and Partnership Plan

They have 30 members in total: Two legislative co-chairs, Members of the Governor's cabinet. Representatives include:

- Large and small firms in cybersecurity
- Businesses likely to be targeted for cyber crime
- Business associations
- Health care and crime victim associations

- Higher education
- The government

In addition, the **National Governors Association** announced the creation of an organization in October 2012 called the **Resource Center for State Cybersecurity** to help states and their agencies guard against cybersecurity threats. The resource center is led by Maryland Gov. Martin O'Malley and Michigan Gov. Rick Snyder. "The overall goal of the Resource Center is to help governors create the most robust policy environment possible to protect our infrastructure, our government and our citizens from cyber threats and data breaches."

There is also a newly created **Baltimore-Washington Cyber Task Force** that was formed in May that will partner with a number of public and private sector organizations to develop and to begin implementing a strategy for cyber industry growth around the activities of CYBERCOM at Ft. Meade.

Director of Cyber Development: The Governor appoint a "director" that will "lead the Administration's efforts to position Maryland as the epicenter of cybersecurity activity, supporting product development, education and talent; working to attract new cyber companies and investors to Maryland; encouraging the continued expansion of cybersecurity programs and assisting start-up cyber firms." The director is Jeani Park.

Centers / Facilities

bwtech@UMBC Cyber Incubator

- Offers business and technical support to early stage Cyber Security companies
- Several cyber companies currently reside in the incubator on UMBC's campus

- Home to the CyberMap, a directory of Cyber companies in Maryland, and the CyberHive, a co-working space dedicated to Cyber Security companies

Cyber Incubator companies

- Alpha Omega Technologies
- Appistry
- ASET Partners
- Ayasdi, Inc.
- Bandura, LLC
- Calvert Systems Engineering
- CWR Technologies
- Cyber Security Engineering Associates (CSEA)
- CyberHive/CyberMap
- DB Networks
- EnDepth Solutions
- ENG Solutions
- Fearless Solutions
- Group Z
- Intellibit
- iWebGate
- KoolSpan
- LightGrid
- Light Point Security
- NETWAR DEFENSE
- Radiant Infotech
- Secured Sciences Group
- SpotKick (BankLook.com)
- TargetGov
- Technology Security Associates
- Tiresias Technologies
- Veris Group

Chesapeake Innovation Center

- Incubator that partners with corporate and government partners to identify technology solutions to mission critical problems
- Recently added a Health IT support to traditional security and defense focus

CyberMaryland

- Public/private partnership organized by the Maryland Department of Business and Economic Development (DBED) that offers resources and services to Cyber companies
- Curator of the CyberMaryland Map and publisher of the CyberMaryland Report
- CyberMaryland Conference facilitates interaction with industry leaders and emerging technologies

The CYNC Program at bwtech@UMBC

- Partnership with Northrop Grumman to commercialize Cyber Security technology
- Provides access to Northrop Grumman representatives and incubator resources

The GroundFloor

- Co-working space opened in 2013 to facilitate commercialization with nearby Aberdeen Proving Ground
- Collaboration with other regional incubators encourages partnerships across the corridor

National Cyber Security Center of Excellence

- Strives to increase the rate of adoption of secure technology
- Advances the Cyber Security industry and accelerates effective innovation
- Develops practical Cyber solutions based on commercially available technology

Universities

Universities, community colleges and technical institutes offering degrees or certificates

- Bowie State
- Capital College
- Johns Hopkins
- Towson University
- US Naval Academy
- University of Maryland Baltimore County
- University of Maryland, College Park
- University of Maryland University College
- Anne Arundel Community College
- College of Southern Maryland
- Hagerstown Community College
- Hartford Community College
- Montgomery College
- Prince George's Community College
- The Community College of Baltimore County
- ITT Tech

Companies

There are currently more than 11,000 companies in Maryland that create products and services to protect against cyber attacks, including Northrop Grumman, JHU APL, Verizon, Lockheed, Booz Allen, SAIC, CSC, BD Diagnostics, Allegis Group, and AAI.

Other Notations

Nearby federal agencies and institutions offer a significant strategic advantage. For example, they are located by:

- NIST

- CYBERCOM

- NSA/CSS

- NASA High Performance Computing Center-2: schedule for completion in 2016 to be located at Ft. Meade.

Venture Capital Deals: 374 from 2008-2012 in cybersecurity valued at $2,096,999,000.

Colleges and universities in the Baltimore-Washington corridor are widely recognized for their ability to consistently train graduates with the tools for success needed in the Cyber Security industry. Five four-year colleges and universities in Greater Baltimore have been recognized by the NSA as excellent institutions for education and research in information assurance.

The Greater Baltimore area is one of the most concentrated markets in the US, with **42% more of its employment concentrated in Cyber Security occupations than the US average.** There are over 75,000 employed in Cyber Security-related jobs in the Greater Baltimore/Central Maryland region, nearly 20,000 open Cyber Security job positions in Maryland, and over 13,000 of available jobs are located in Greater Baltimore.

They also put on the **CyberMaryland conference.** This year's conference was this week (Oct 8 - 9) and featured speakers such as Kathleen Rice (Counsel, Senate Select Committee on Intelligence), Kristina Dorville (DHS), and various industry and university representatives.

MASSACHUSETTS

Massachusetts has a very high level of cybersecurity activity and should likely be considered as one of the model states regarding IA/CD capability. The state has standard cybersecurity, cyberbullying, and identity theft laws and a fairly active state government that recognizes and supports the advancement of cybersecurity as a strategic need. The state shines particularly bright in its research and education sectors. The state is home to two major cybersecurity research organizations with the MITRE Corporation's Bedford location and Lincoln Labs at MIT. There are many other smaller centers, organizations, and working groups operating in both industry and academia. The state has a truly massive education system offering both advanced research and cybersecurity education options that lead to degrees or certificates. The state has four NSA Centers of Excellence and two major Ivy League institutions at Harvard and MIT. The academic institutions are massively funded through federal grants and are engaged in nearly every foreseeable cybersecurity research area spanning the technical and policy divide. In sum, the state appears to be a thought-leader with enormous research and practice output. The state should be included in the highest category regarding cybersecurity activity.

State / Policy Activities

Massachusetts has a relatively robust data breach notification law on their books and the state hosts a cybersecurity specific webpage offering links, best practices, and guidance. The state also appears to have enacted laws specifically targeting cyberbullying, online stalking, and identity theft.

https://malegislature.gov/Laws/GeneralLaws/PartI/TitleXV/Chapter93 H & http://www.mass.gov/anf/research-and-tech/cyber-security/

The state is one of six in the US that has developed and utilizes the Cyber Aces (http://www.cyberaces.org/) program. The program is a cybersecurity talent development effort using competitions to select promising students for cybersecurity education and internship opportunities. The program is described as…*Cyber Aces State Championship, an online* competition to recruit high school and college students as well as members of the military into the field of cybersecurity, kicked off Thursday. The state is partnering with Cyber Aces, a non-profit educational and workplace training group with programs in six states including Massachusetts, New York, and New Jersey focusing on areas like networking fundamentals, operating systems and secure system administration.

http://wamc.org/post/mass-addressing-cybersecurity-needs

The announcement for the program from the governor can be found at http://www.mass.gov/governor/administration/councilscabinetsandcommissions/military/ma-cyber-aces-kickoff.html

The state also hosts one of America's Federal Reserve banks in Boston.

Centers / Facilities

There two major cybersecurity research facilities and many smaller specialized academic centers operating in the state of Massachusetts. The two major research entities are the MITRE Corporation in Bedford and Lincoln Labs at the Massachusetts Institute of Technology (MIT). The MITRE Corporation has cybersecurity as one of its core capability and their activities are too numerous to detail here. But specifically in Massachusetts there is the Advanced Cyber Security Center (ACSC).

The center is described in the following passage. The Advanced Cyber Security Center (ACSC) *is a non-profit corporation launched and supported by Mass Insight Global Partnerships that brings together industry, university, and government partners to address sophisticated cyber security challenges. By drawing on expertise from across health care, energy, defense, financial services and technology, the ACSC brings together experts to develop unique approaches to share cyber threat information, to engage in next-generation cyber security research and development, and to create education programs that develop cyber security talent. The ACSC, based at The MITRE Corporation campus in Bedford, MA, takes advantage of New England's unparalleled university, industrial and research resources to develop next-generation solutions and strategies for protecting the nation's public and private IT infrastructure.*

http://www.massinsight.com/initiatives/cyber_security_center/

Additionally, the Center is advertised in the following way… *Touted as a first of its kind collaborative effort that brings together stakeholders in cyber security from the government, industry and academia, the ACSC is also hosted at the five universities that make up the Massachusetts Green High Performance Computing Center – MIT, Harvard University, Boston University, Northeastern University and the University of Massachusetts.*

http://www.bizjournals.com/boston/blog/mass-high-tech/2011/09/new-cyber-security-center-launches-to-help.html?page=all

The state's enormous education system has taken a number of collaborative efforts with relevance to cybersecurity. For example, *the Massachusetts Green High Performance Computing Center (MGHPCC) is a data center dedicated to research computing. It is operated by five of the most research-intensive universities in Massachusetts: Boston University, Harvard University, MIT, Northeastern University, and the University of Massachusetts. It serves the growing research computing needs of the five founding universities as well as other research institutions.*

http://www.mghpcc.org/

Lincoln Labs at MIT is the state's resident national laboratory and focuses heavily on cybersecurity and high technology research.

https://www.ll.mit.edu/mission/communications/cyber/cybersecurity.html

Universities

Massachusetts has an enormous education system and many of those schools are carrying out cybersecurity research and education. Suffice to say, it is not feasible to cover all the areas, universities, and projects currently underway in Massachusetts. Instead, the content below will serve as an overview with specific highlights designed to show the breadth and depth of Massachusetts' scholarly work in IA/CD.

There are four NSA Centers of Academic Excellence in Massachusetts: Boston University, Northeastern University, Worcester Polytechnic University, and University of Massachusetts – Amherst.

Additionally, Massachusetts is home to two of the nation's most prestigious and technically advanced universities in Harvard and MIT.

Harvard has many faculty, centers, and departments engaged in IA/CD research and practice. There is the Berkman Center for Internet and Society (http://cyber.law.harvard.edu/) which is known for privacy work, legal scholarship, and studying emerging technology. Since 2010, the Berkman Center has been developing and maintaining a cybersecurity wiki

http://cyber.law.harvard.edu/cybersecurity/Main_Page.

Additionally, the following centers do work of import to information assurance: Harvard Business School, the Belfer Center, and the Kennedy School of Government. Unsurprisingly, the Computer Science department works on security as a research area of interest but does not offer specialized degree options. In the computer science department there is…*Harvard's Center for Research on Computation and Society (CRCS) brings computer scientists together with a broad range of scholars from other fields to develop new computer science theory and technology in the public interest, informed by a deep knowledge of the societal issues at stake. Areas of study include healthcare informatics, electronic markets, privacy, security, and social computing.*

http://crcs.seas.harvard.edu/

There is a pronounced focus on the issue of privacy in much of Harvard's security related research.

http://dataprivacylab.org/

MIT is engaged in a fairly enormous amount of cybersecurity research and practice. For a broad overview see http://cybersecurity.mit.edu/. MIT has researchers and academics working on the following security challenges:

cloud security, privacy, big data, network security, virtualization, smart grid security, mobile malware and virtually any topic imaginable. In MIT's Electric Engineering and Computer Science (EECS) department there is considerable work on security being performed by the Computer Science and Artificial Intelligence Lab (CSAIL) http://css.csail.mit.edu/. In the CSAIL center there is a cryptography and information security working group doing both research and teaching courses on network security and cryptography.

http://toc.csail.mit.edu/?q=node/46

There are many courses of IA/CD relevance taught throughout the MIT system but they do not appear to offer undergraduate or graduate cybersecurity degree programs. They also offer learning opportunities via professional and continuing educations.

http://web.mit.edu/professional/short-programs/courses/applied_cyber_security.html

The following institutions offering varying cybersecurity degree options: Bay Path University, Boston University, Worcester Polytechnic, University of Massachusetts, Northeastern University, Mass Bay Community College, Brandeis, and many affiliate universities in the University of Massachusetts system.

For overview information on Massachusetts educational options see http://www.acscenter.org/news-events/cyber_security_resource_directory_2011.pdf.

Companies

Massachusetts is a relative tech center of gravity. This is partly due to the reality of Boston as an economically powerful metropolis and the enormous size and funding of the universities in Massachusetts. That said it's not reasonable to enumerate all the cybersecurity relevant corporations, companies, and bodies operating within Massachusetts. The state has companies with cybersecurity missions in all the major sectors like finance, defense, tech, government, healthcare, and energy.

Below is a list of some of the companies with a presence in Massachusetts. This list is taken from the partners section of the Advanced Cyber Security Center's website.

- Akamai
- Biogen Idec
- Bit9
- Blue Cross Blue Shield of Massachusetts
- Boston University
- Broad Institute
- Commonwealth of Massachusetts
- Confer Technologies
- Courion
- Draper Laboratory
- Eastern Bank
- Facebook
- Federal Reserve Bank of Boston
- Foley Hoag LLP
- Harvard University

- Harvard Pilgrim Health Care
- John Hancock Financial Services, Inc.
- Liberty Mutual Group
- MIT
- MIT Lincoln Laboratory
- Northeastern University
- Pfizer Inc.
- RSA, The Security Division of EMC
- State Street Corporation
- The MITRE Corporation
- University of Massachusetts
- Veracode
- Worcester Polytechnic Institute

MICHIGAN

Michigan considers itself a showcase for a national model for public/private partnerships addressing cyber security for its businesses, residents. The state was one of the initial collaborators on a multiple university internet system. Michigan has capitalized on this early entry into technology to support MERIT and have well-integrated partnerships with all levels of government, the private sector and education. There is a well-designed strategic state initiative with a professional and easy to use internet presence Michigan Cyber Initiative. Michigan Cyber Range and Merit have invested in an informational websites in support of their message. The Governor has hosted 3 cybersecurity conferences and there is a strong focus on educating all sectors of the public

State / Policy Activities

Michigan has a long standing tradition of building and maintaining collaborative internet/security relationships. The legislature passed three cybersecurity laws, Identity Theft Protection Act 452, Social Security Number Privacy Act and the Michigan Anti-spam laws. The Office of the Governor has hosted sold out cyber summits in 2011 and 2013. The third Cyber Summit is being advertised as the North American International Cyber Summit 2014. The previous two events have sold out and attendance fees of $99 and $79for 2014 will encourage another 'sold out' event. These summits have strong corporate sponsorship.

The State is pulling together a $3 billion private public initiative, "Pure Michigan Business Connect" to promote entrepreneurship to capital and a 'cyber security business environment. The Michigan Economic Development Corporation (MEDC) is the state's marketing arm to attract businesses and encourage economic growth with tax free zones. Cybersecurity was mentioned in an early 2005 initiative, restated in 2014 and has been supported by Merit.

Centers / Facilities

Michigan has a number of active coalitions and organizations: Washtenaw County Cyber Citizenship Coalition, Merit, Michigan Cyber Civilian Corps (MiC3). These organizations are non-profit and/or volunteer organizations modeling the state initiative to provide well-integrated partnership. Early internet development seeded Merit Network

Merit Network, Inc., (inception 1966) started building network connections between Michigan universities prior to the internet and has continued as a non-profit organization to expand its coalition and reach to include Illinois, Ohio, Wisconsin and Minnesota. Accomplishment include REACH-3MC, 2,287 miles of 2,287 miles of open-access, advanced fiber-optic network through rural and underserved communities in Michigan's Lower and Upper Peninsulas, and a robust cybersecurity curriculum comprised of 22 certification programs offered hybrid on-line/in class. Merit Network, Inc., a consortium of Michigan universities, and the State of Michigan, as well as two commercial companies, IBM and MCI. Merit Research has a long list of NSF and Defense funded projects and collaborations with out-of-state universities.

Michigan Information Sharing and Analysis Center addresses state's cyber security readiness and critical infrastructure coordination led by State's IT Department and modeled after the NCCIC at DHS.

Michigan Intelligence Operation Center (MIOC) is the statewide Fusion Center and has a well-illustrated page on their website drawing the connection to Michigan Intelligence Operations Center and the Michigan Cyber Defense Response Team. The Michigan Cyber Command Center is under development.

Universities

Michigan has five centers of academic excellence and research: Davenport University, Eastern Michigan University, Ferris State University,

University of Detroit, Mercy, Walsh College. Central Michigan and Davenport universities also offers CSIA degree and courses.

Companies

Sponsors for the Michigan State conference include companies such as AT&T, Deloitt, Comcast, Symantec, Unisys, IBM, Cisco, MicroSoft, Motorola, ITC, Sprint, Tenable Network Security, Security Mentor, Merit and Century Link, Ford Motor Company, URS Corporation, CyberCoders, and other companies including, but not limited to, Adva Optical Networking, Cisco Systems, Data Strategy, and Juniper Networks have a presence in Michigan and are represented as being involved in the collaborative public/private partnership arrangements.

Other Notations

Michigan's governor has hosted to 'Michigan Cyber Summits – 2011, 2013 – in conjunction with Cybersecurity month. The Summit is a partnership between levels of local, state and federal government such as the Washtenaw County Cyber Citizenship Coalition, State of Michigan Office of the Governor and the National Governors Association as well as many private partners.

Michigan was involved in the DHS - EINSTEIN initiative to conduct a proof of concept. Michigan is currently involved in second phase of this initiative, ALBERT. The plan is to roll EINSTEIN out nationally.

1) http://www.uscybersecurity.net/Pages/current_online_magazine.html

   - Pure Michigan is another marketing effort to bring attention, highlight initiatives and create "buzz" to encourage businesses to choose Michigan as a place to do business.

2) Michigan Cyber Initiative is informative and well-constructed website

3) http://bxjmag.com/growing-opportunities-in-the-cybersecurity-economy/ Insights into MEDC

4) EINSTEIN provides US-CERT a situational awareness snapshot of the health of the federal governments' cyber space. Based upon agreements with participating federal agencies, US-CERT installs systems at their Internet access points to collect network flow data. The agencies are provided tools to analyze their collected data. In addition, the data is shared with US-CERT Security Operations Center, which aggregates it from all EINSTEIN participants to identify network anomalies spanning the federal government.

MINNESOTA

The State through the collaboration with the non-profit organization, Advance IT Minnesota, is positioning Minnesota as a top-ten regional economy for information technology careers as measured by total IT-related employment. Through a strong quality education system which has increased enrollment in IT 76% since 2006. Four state colleges, universities are Centers for Academic Excellence. The state has taken a systemic approach to bringing K-20, academia, government and industry together to support their mission.

http://advanceitmn.org/about

State / Policy Activities

In 1991 Minnesota consolidated the post-secondary system under one chancellor and governing board consisting of 31 institutions on 54 campuses in 47 communities. The schools report job placement rate at two-year colleges is 92.6 percent, meaning that 92.6 percent of graduates find jobs quickly in their chosen fields.[1] This same level of 'planned excellence' appears to have transferred to the CAE/cyber security educational system.

Last year Minnesota Department of Commerce completed a state-wide survey of cybersecurity practices[2] of small and medium sized businesses. The state demonstrates a high level of performance

Centers / Facilities

Technological Leadership Institute is affiliated with the University of Minnesota and has sponsored the Cybersecurity Summit for the past four years.

---

[1] http://en.wikipedia.org/wiki/Minnesota_State_Colleges_and_Universities_System
[2] http://mn.gov/commerce/images/CyberSecurityResults14.pdf

Universities

Minnesota is the home of six designated Centers of Academic Excellence: Inver Hills Community College and Minneapolis Community and Technical College are CAE/2Y. Capella University, Metropolitan State University, St Cloud State University and the University of Minnesota are all CAE/IAE.

Companies

- MWW Group
- Atomic Data
- LuciData Group
- CRGT
- Target
- Caylor
- PwC
- General Mills
- United Health Group
- Honeywell
- ATK

- Stroz Friedberg
- Ameriprize Financial
- Alliant TechSystems Inc.
- Best Buys
- Univita Health
- Carlson Rezidor Hotel Group
- Bluestem Brands, Inc.
- Ameriprise
- Alliant Tech Systems Inc.

Other Notations

1) http://advanceitmn.org/about Advance Minnesota IT

2) http://advanceitmn.org/offerings

3) MN has a put on a 2 ½ day cybersecurity summit: the event is focused on changing how digital space and security are approached. The summit takes a multi-stakeholder consortium consisting of industry, government and academia.

4) http://minnesotabusiness.com/cyber-security-summit

5) http://mn.gov/commerce/images/CybersecuritySummary14.pdf

MISSISSIPPI

The State's claim to fame is Mississippi State University (MSSU) - ranked by the Ponemon Institute as the third best university to study cybersecurity in the country. For a state of its size, Mississippi has a fair share of military installations; Kessler AFB plus the other four installations and the Stennis Space Center draw a fair amount of government and cybersecurity activity/awareness.

State / Policy Activities

The State's cybersecurity profile and prominence is tied closely with the success and maturity of MSSU. The State has updated their cyber-crimes, cyber bullying and cyber stalking laws. The website is clearly laid out a policies are up-to-date. The state and MSSU has close ties to the FBI and DHS. While the state doesn't make loud noises as being a leader in cybersecurity, for a 'small' state with one major university, Mississippi is well positioned in the cyber law enforcement lane.

Centers / Facilities

Mississippi has a fair number of military installations:

- Columbus and Kessler AFB
- Camp Shelby Army Base
- Navy's Gulfport Battalion Center
- Naval Air Station (NAS) Meridian
- Stennis Space Center

Universities

Mississippi State University is the only university ranked as a CAE in Mississippi; but the school holds all three designations, CAE, CAE-R and IA. The University has a strong reputation for digital forensics and working with veterans, collaborating with the FBI, DHS and other three letter agencies.

Companies

- Apex
- APP Labs
- Batesville Casket Company
- Bowhead
- Computer Science Corporation
- Information Innovators
- Lockheed Martin
- Mainline Information Systems
- Medical Transportation Management
- Mindseekers, Inc.
- Morpho Trust
- NetApps
- Raytheon
- SAKS Incorporated
- SpectorSoft
- Think Anew
- Triple I

Other Notations

1) Ponemon ranking of MSSU
   http://www.msstate.edu/web/media/detail.php?id=6502

2) http://www.its.ms.gov/Services/Pages/services_security.aspx

3) http://www.ago.state.ms.us/divisions/cyber-crime/

4) http://www.olemiss.edu/depts/ncjrl/pdf/CyberCrimebooklet.pdf

MISSOURI

Missouri appears to be an innovative educationally, but the state was not an early adaptor of cyber legislation. Having Scott Air Force Base, being part of the Cyber Security Education Consortium and having Boeing located in the St. Louis area has strengthened cybersecurity prominence in the state. The State has a clear mission for cyber and puts a straight forward message as expressed on the State website.

State / Policy Activities

Missouri's Mission for cybersecurity is to promote and provide expertise in information security management for all state agencies and support national and local homeland information security efforts. Their Vision is to be a leader in preserving the confidentiality, integrity, and availability of state data and dependent resources while maintaining efficient and effective operations.

Missouri passed cyber bullying and cyber stalking legislation in 2013.

Centers / Facilities

In 2012 Scott AFB established the Joint Cyber Center to address persistent and increasing cyber attacks on transportation systems.

Center for Cyber Security Research is located at the University of Missouri – Columbia.

Universities

Missouri has two centers of academic excellence, Missouri University of Science and Technology (CAE/IAE, CAE/R and the University of Missouri- Columbia, a CAE/IAE.

Other schools offering cyber security degrees include Fontebonne University, a cyber security major, Southeast Missouri State University offers and Southwestern Missouri and Missouri State University offer a 12 hour graduate certificate. Washington University is offering a new degree in Cybersecurity Management. Washington University developed a Master degree in Information Management and Cybersecurity in 2013 "designed to fill the need to be able to secure the business without hobbling the business."

Missouri is a member of the Cyber Security Education Consortium "a cohesive partnership of community colleges and career and technology centers in Arkansas, Colorado, Kansas, Louisiana, Tennessee and Texas. St, Louis Community College offers a program in network security and Metropolitan Community College offers two year AA degrees.

Companies

Businesses and organizations:

- Car Fax
- Mycroft

Major corporations:

- Boeing
- IBM
- L3 Communications
- Booz Allen Hamilton
- CACI International
- Co-Sentry
- Honeywell
- MasterCard provide employment in Missouri in cybersecurity fields

MONTANA

Montana's cybersecurity activity is relatively low to moderate compared to other states. They have data breach laws, a relatively engaged state government, and s small offering of cybersecurity programs. Montana lacks the size and funding resources of other more active states and they lack diversity and options for cybersecurity education and employment. In general, their posture places them in the low or middle echelons of state-level cybersecurity activity.

State / Policy Activities

Montana has a standard data breach notification laws (2-6-504. Notification of breach of security of data system & MONT CODE ANN § 30-14-1704: Montana Code - Section 30-14-1704: Computer security breach) that can be found at

http://leg.mt.gov/bills/mca/2/6/2-6-504.htm.

The state government provides a relatively exhaustive information security webpage (http://infosec.mt.gov/default.mcpx) and the state does have a CISO position as of 2013. Montana is in the process of accelerating their cybersecurity efforts with some details provided in this interview article

http://www.govtech.com/blogs/lohrmann-on-cybersecurity/Elevating-cybersecurity-leadership-Perspectives-from-Montanas-CIO-and-CISO.html

Centers / Facilities

Montana does not host any major cybersecurity research centers (national labs, FFRDCs, etc.) and the bulk of their research on IA is being performed by academics.

Universities

Montana is one of a just a handful of states that do not have any NSA approved centers of excellence and Montana's education system does not provide a large number of options for cybersecurity education. University of Montana (UM) is offering course work and engaged in projects to boost their cybersecurity curriculum. Earlier this year, using NSF funding UM created a new Cyber Innovation Laboratory dubbed "Cyberlab" that is focused on IA and other relevant tech topics. Cyberlab is described on http://www.umt.edu/cyberlab/default.php as follows...*The purpose of the lab is to provide a collaborative space to support undergraduate and graduate students, faculty, researchers, guest speakers, and community business partners in their studies of Big Data Analytics, Information Assurance, and Cyber Security Forensics. Opened in January, 2014, the lab is designed to provide hardware and software in an isolated computing environment that fosters experiential learning, creativity, and discovery.*

UM's Cyberlab also hosts a Cyber Triathlon event that lets students compete on various technology puzzles including IA challenges. The Triathlon is described on their site in the following way...*On May 3, high-school and college students from around the state gathered at the University of Montana to compete. The challenge included a digital forensics puzzle, a data analytics puzzle and a hacking puzzle. The goal of the competition was to find a "coin" hidden somewhere on the University of Montana campus. The first team to solve all three parts of the Cyber Triathlon and find the Cyber Coin won!*

UM does not offer specific cybersecurity degree programs but they do off a cybersecurity certificate program...The Network and Information Security Professional Certificate is designed to prepare computer and networking professionals for a career in the emerging field of computer security by providing advanced experience in the areas of business continuity, computer system design, contingency planning, data integrity, risk assessment and mitigation techniques, security investigation, and troubleshooting.

http://www.umt.edu/cyberlab/cyber-security-courses.php

The University of Montana is starting courses in cyber security using big data in its new Cyber Innovation Laboratory funded by a $500,000 grant from the National Science Foundation and another $40,000 from local technology companies.

http://www.fiercebigdata.com/story/university-montana-opens-new-big-data-cyber-security-courses/2013-11-05

Missoula College, a two-year college in Montana was recently approved to start teaching a computer security certificate program... *"This involves learning how to hack, how to stop hackers, how to repair the damage that has been done and how to build systems that protect people from hackers in the future,"* said *University of Montana Provost Perry Brown*. *"They'll learn all those skills and go into a business and work with them to make sure their networks and systems are as prepared as possible."*

http://missoulian.com/news/state-and-regional/regents-ok-missoula-college-to-offer-computer-security-certificate-program/article_ba37d196-78d4-11e3-b66a-0019bb2963f4.html

Other than the above mentioned programs there is little other evidence of a large cybersecurity education effort occurring in Montana.

Companies

Montana does not have a large specialized cybersecurity industry. There are a number of small boutique security and analytics companies that have taken advantage of Montana's low cost of living. For example,

http://lmgsecurity.com/ and http://teradact.com/index.html.

Montana has recognized the need for partnership and engagement in developing their IT industry

http://www.missoulapartnership.com/sector-strengths/information-technology/.

NEBRASKA

Nebraska has a moderately high level of cybersecurity activity. They have fairly strong data breach laws, a proactive state government, and a small but energetic group of researchers, academics, and educators working on cybersecurity. Their state government has a good reputation and hosts conferences and is active in outreach and organizing. Their educational posture is limited in size but there two CAEs with developed security programs. There are no major labs or R&D centers but academics are engaged in specialized studies in university centers. The industry around cybersecurity is not particularly developed but there are some bright spots. In general, Nebraska is likely "punching above its weight" on cybersecurity and is firmly in the middle echelon.

State / Policy Activities

Nebraska has a fairly standard and robust set of data breach notification laws with their Nebraska Revised Statute 87-801:807 that were first enacted in 2006. The state has a published IS policy updated as of 2013 that can be found at http://nitc.nebraska.gov/standards/8-101.html

The state has a specific but limited cybersecurity web presence with http://www.cio.nebraska.gov/cyber-sec/index.html. Nebraska appears to be relatively active in community outreach and cybersecurity organizing at the state level. Their CISO has a solid reputation for getting things done and has served in leadership positions with NASCIO and engaged in other collaborative efforts to strengthen state and community cybersecurity. Nebraska has recently hosted some cybersecurity conferences and events such as the 2014 NACo National Cyber Symposium in Omaha, Nebraska and the annual Nebraska Cyber Security Conference. Generally speaking, Nebraska has a fairly active cybersecurity posture with an emphasis on collaboration and outreach.

Centers / Facilities

Nebraska does not have the national labs or FFRDCs found in other states but their academic community appears to be relatively active and cooperative in cybersecurity studies. For example, at the University of Nebraska Lincoln there is partnership activity and specialized institutes interested in security. Specifically, at Nebraska Lincoln... *University of Nebraska President James B. Milliken announced Feb. 12 that NU has signed an agreement with the Indian Institute of Technology Delhi, one of the world's leading technology institutes, to collaborate on research and education in the critical areas of information assurance and cybersecurity.*

http://www.unomaha.edu/college-of-information-science-and-technology/engagement/centers/nebraska-university-center-for-information-assurance/index.php

Also, at Nebraska Lincoln there is the Peter Kiewit Institute which has broad technology interests including security, from their website... *Information assurance (IA) is an emerging and rapidly expanding area of study which addresses fundamental problems in the design, development, implementation and support of secure information systems. The need for secure information systems has become a paramount concern as the computer-enabled, Internet-connected, digital-based global society of the 21st century emerges. The college offers an undergraduate degree program in IA (BS in IA). In addition, students pursuing their undergraduate (BS) degrees in Computer Science or Management Information Systems can chose an IA area of concentration.*

Additionally there is the CSFI, description from their site... *The Cyber Security Forum Initiative (CSFI) is a non-profit organization headquartered in Omaha, NE and in Washington DC with a mission "to provide Cyber Warfare awareness, guidance, and security solutions through collaboration, education, volunteer work, and training to assist the US Government, US Military, Commercial Interests, and International Partners." CSFI was born out of the collaboration of dozens of experts, and today CSFI is comprised of a large community of nearly 25,000 Cyber Security and Cyber Warfare professionals from the government, military, private sector, and academia. Our amazing members are the core of all of our activities, and it is for them that we are pushing forward our mission.*

http://www.csfi.us/?page=about

Universities

There are two NSA approved CAEs at the University of Nebraska at Omaha (UNO) and Bellevue University. At UNO there is the Nebraska University Center for Information Assurance (NUCIA) with the following description taken from

http://www.unomaha.edu/college-of-information-science-and-technology/engagement/centers/nebraska-university-center-for-information-assurance/index.php.

Since its founding in 2001, the Nebraska University Center for Information Assurance (NUCIA) has helped improve the posture of information assurance awareness locally, regionally and nationally. The collaborative efforts of faculty, students and community partners have earned UNO the distinction of being named a Center of Academic Excellence in Information Assurance Education by the National Security Agency (NSA).

UN Omaha offers two major degrees in cybersecurity with a BS and MS in Information Assurance and a certificate in Information Assurance targeting working professionals and graduates.

Bellevue University is the other CAE offering a BS-Cybersecurity degree. Hosted at Bellevue University is the Center for Cybersecurity Education (CCE) which according to their website -- *offers a wide variety of interdisciplinary degrees, student resources, and community outreach events. The Center brings together the best cybersecurity education programs with highly qualified faculty who possess the kind of real world experience you expect at Bellevue University."*

Companies

Aside from the ubiquitous military industrial complex companies that work in cybersecurity and a number of smaller information security consultancies there are not many large specialized cybersecurity firms in Nebraska.

NEVADA

Nevada has some relatively unique characteristics concerning cybersecurity. Firstly, the state has some of the more stringent data breach and data security laws on its books. Particularly, Nevada has mandated PCI-DSS for companies operating in the state with payment cards. Secondly, Nevada is made unique by the enormous gaming industry centered around Las Vegas and to a lesser extent Reno. Nevada has one NSA center of academic excellence with the University of Nevada Las Vegas and has a number of state universities offering research and learning opportunities in the field of cybersecurity. The State's historic proximity to nuclear energy and weapons adds another unique facet to their cybersecurity posture. Ultimately, Nevada's cybersecurity profile likely lacks some of the size and breadth seen in states like California or Maryland.

State / Policy Activities

Nevada has a relatively basic data breach notification law on their books with revisions in 2010 and 2011 but they have added two provisions strengthening their statutory requirements. Firstly, Nevada has codified PCI-DSS into their data security laws. The below is an excerpt from an online article:

> *Two other states have incorporated all or parts of PCI DSS into state law include Minnesota (with the Plastic Card Security Act in 2007) and Nevada (with Nev. Rev. Stat. Ch. 603A that became effective in 2010). Nevada's law requires "data collectors," including government agencies and businesses, that accept payment cards and are "doing business" in Nevada to comply with the Payment Card Industry Data Security Standard ("PCI DSS"). Although Minnesota has codified the PCI DSS requirement that prohibits businesses from retaining certain credit or debit card data after a transaction, Nevada now becomes the only state to require compliance with PCI DSS in its entirety.*

The new Nevada law prohibits electronically transmitting a customer's personal information "outside of the secure system of the business" or moving any data storage device containing a customer's personal information "beyond the logical or physical controls" of the business unless the transmission or data storage device is encrypted.

Nevada also has a CISO position with an Office of Information Security located in their Enterprise IT department. This organization offers advice and guidance via their webpage. The Nevada Attorney General also offers best practices information and since 1999 Nevada has had a Technological Crime Advisory Board that focuses to some degree on electronic crimes like identity theft, online, fraud, etc. Nevada has an Emergency Management department with a Homeland Security office and the state is home to four fusion centers that work with DHS and other intelligence and security agencies. Nevada derives considerable money from the gaming industry and there appears to be considerable information security interest displayed the gaming industry. Information is not particularly easy to come by but recently the Nevada Gaming Policy Commission has convened for the first time in decades to discuss the challenges presented by online gaming and its security.

Centers / Facilities

I can find no mention of FFRDCs located in Nevada in the NSF master list. Historically, Nevada has been very involved in nuclear testing and nuclear security and some of these agencies have limited cybersecurity R&D mission sets related to protecting the nuclear stockpile and weapon design information. Agencies such as the National Nuclear Security Administration work in this space. Many groups have managed or operated at the famous Nevada Test Site, currently a consortium of companies with military industrial and energy interests operate the site with former tenants being the Bechtel Company and Lockheed Martin.

Universities

The University of Nevada, Reno is establishing the Cyber Security Center…"We will be taking a holistic approach to cyber security, blending the technical aspects of protecting cyberspace with a range of disciplines from business to the liberal arts." "[The center] will work on solutions to cyber attacks, educate students and conduct relevant research. The multiple faculty disciplines involved include computer science and engineering, political science, information studies, journalism, criminal justice, mathematics, philosophy, psychology and military science." *The proposed Cyber Security Center received support from the Northern Nevada Regional Intelligence Center, Washoe County Sheriff's Office, Nevada Governor's Office of Economic Development, National Security Forum, EDAWN and local digital forensics company Vere Software. The center will include close collaborations with the Desert Research Institute and the University of Nevada, Las Vegas.*

UNLV School of Informatics offers multiple cyber specialization tracks like digital forensics, network forensics, and cybersecurity. It is also recognized as a NSA CAE and is the only CAE in Nevada. The College of Southern Nevada, offers primarily two-year degrees with a number of courses bearing relevance to information security (electronic crime investigation, network security, etc.).

Companies

The enormous gaming industry has considerable interest in cybersecurity but specific information is not particularly easy to come by since the companies are highly competitive. The defense industry also maintains facilities in Nevada providing consulting and R&D services (CACI, Lockheed, etc.).

Other Notations

The gaming industry's approach to cybersecurity could be an interesting avenue for study but is likely too broad for inclusion in this profile document. Perhaps, we should include the tribal gaming associations in future discussion on securing personal information and financial assets.

Casey: Nevada, New Hampshire, New Jersey, New Mexico, North Carolina, Ohio.

Guiding Questions

1) Legislation at the state level in the area of cybersecurity.

    a. Data Breach notification law signed 2011. Pretty standard.

    b. Two other states have incorporated all or parts of PCI DSS into state law include Minnesota (with the Plastic Card Security Act in 2007) and Nevada (with Nev. Rev. Stat. Ch. 603A that became effective in 2010).

    c. Nevada's law requires "data collectors," including government agencies and businesses, that accept payment cards and are "doing business" in Nevada to comply with the Payment Card Industry Data Security Standard ("PCI DSS"). Although Minnesota has codified the PCI DSS requirement that prohibits businesses from retaining certain credit or debit card data after a transaction, Nevada now becomes the only state to require compliance with PCI DSS in its entirety.

    d. The new Nevada law prohibits electronically transmitting a customer's personal information "outside of the secure system of the business" or moving any data storage device containing a customer's personal information "beyond the logical or physical controls" of the business unless the transmission or data storage device is encrypted.

    e. The Technological Crime Advisory Board was created by legislation in 1999

    f. Nevada AG maintains webpage with information security information and links but limited

    g. State Government also has an Enterprise IT department with an office of information security that has information and lists the State's policies, procedures, and guidelines.

    h. State has a CISO

> > i. http://it.nv.gov/governance/state-policy-procedures/
>
> i. Has state Emergency Management office with a HS component and four fusion centers located in the state.
> j. Nevada's Gaming Policy Committee has recognized challenges associated with cybersecurity and online gaming and traditional gaming.
>
> > i. Verifying age, location, and detecting fraud or cheating
> > ii. Even go so far as detecting and preventing problem gambling
> > iii. Groups of companies seeking NIST funding grants to develop new technologies to support online gaming security

2) Centers of cybersecurity research/practice.
   a. The University of Nevada, Reno is establishing the Cyber Security Center
      i. "We will be taking a holistic approach to cyber security, blending the technical aspects of protecting cyberspace with a range of disciplines from business to the liberal arts,"
      ii. will work on solutions to cyber attacks, educate students and conduct relevant research. The multiple faculty disciplines involved include computer science and engineering, political science, information studies, journalism, criminal justice, mathematics, philosophy, psychology and military science.
      iii. The proposed Cyber Security Center received support from the Northern Nevada Regional

Intelligence Center, Washoe County Sheriff's Office, Nevada Governor's Office of Economic Development, National Security Forum, EDAWN and local digital forensics company Vere Software. The center will include close collaborations with the Desert Research Institute and the University of Nevada, Las Vegas.

    b. UNLV School of Informatics offers multiple cyber specialization tracks like digital forensics, network forensics, and cybersecurity. It is also recognized as a NSA CAE.

    c. College of Southern Nevada, offering primarily two-year degrees with a number of courses bearing relevance to information security (electronic crime investigation, network security, etc.)

3) Technical/analytical cybersecurity facilities in the state.

    a. No FFRDCs listed in the NSF master list

    b. Historically, Nevada has been very involved in nuclear testing and nuclear security and some of these agencies have limited cybersecurity R&D mission sets related to protecting the nuclear stockpile and weapon design information. Agencies such as the National Nuclear Security Administration work in this space.

    c. Many groups have managed or operated at the famous Nevada Test Site, currently a consortium of companies with military industrial and energy interests operate the site with former tenants being the Bechtel Company and Lockheed Martin.

4) What are the state's cybersecurity main research/practice focus(es).

a. The collegiate offerings appear to have no major specialization, instead offering curricula focused on things like network security and forensics.

b. The State has some unique interests stemming from the gaming industry's location in Las Vegas and Reno. Unsurprisingly, the gaming companies are relatively tight-lipped regarding their information security strategies and efforts but with increasing focus accorded to online gaming and high tech fraud there is likely considerable money being applied to cybersecurity in gaming.

5) What funding do they have from the funding agencies (NSF, etc.).

a. The historic relevance of nuclear energy and weapon testing means there is some cooperation between the state of Nevada and its companies/agencies and the US Department of Energy. There are also military facilities that likely focus on cybersecurity but information is hard to source. The State's relatively small size and remoteness suggests that it lacks the ubiquitous research centers and universities located in neighboring California or even New Mexico.

6) http://www.sandia.gov/locations/index.html - Nevada is a location for this NM based company.

NEW HAMPSHIRE

Generally speaking, New Hampshire has a moderate level of cybersecurity activity. They have a number of academic programs teaching cybersecurity and engaging in information assurance research (particularly Dartmouth). The state's efforts are relatively standard including robust data breach notification laws and a state government webpage devoted to cybersecurity. They lack major research centers but Dartmouth College is very engaged in multi-disciplinary cybersecurity studies. Their private sector footprint is relatively small but given the state's modest size their industrial cybersecurity base is respectable. Overall, NH is solidly in the middle when it comes to cybersecurity posture, research, and industry.

State / Policy Activities

New Hampshire has a fairly robust data breach notification law that incorporates many of the elements found in other states throughout the US. NH has a devoted cybersecurity webpage on the state government's Information Technology site offering best practices, guidance, and basic threat alert information. The site can be viewed here:

http://www.nh.gov/doit/cybersecurity/

The state has a hopeful outlook regarding the computer science and cybersecurity industries... *Those seeking jobs in cybersecurity and general computer science fields are pleased to discover that New Hampshire expects to see "professional, scientific, and technical services . . . [to grow] nearly 24 percent" between the years of 2010 and 2020.*

http://www.cybersecurityu.org/new-hampshire-steady-economy-attracts-cyber-professionals/

Centers / Facilities

There are no national laboratories or Federally Funded Research and Development Centers located in New Hampshire. That said, Dartmouth

College developed and currently managed the Institute for Information Infrastructure Protection (I3P). The Institute was created with federal funding with the following mission...

The Institute for Information Infrastructure Protection (I3P) is a consortium of leading universities, national laboratories and nonprofit institutions dedicated to strengthening the cyber infrastructure of the United States.

The Institute for Information Infrastructure Protection—the I3P—is a national consortium of leading academic institutions, national laboratories and non-profit research organizations. Since its founding in 2002, the I3P has been a cornerstone in the coordination of cyber security research and development. The I3P brings together researchers, government officials, and industry representatives to address cyber security challenges affecting the nation's critical infrastructure

http://www.thei3p.org/about/index.html

Universities

New Hampshire has a moderate number of cybersecurity programs being offered at universities in the state. Regarding NSA Centers of Excellence, New Hampshire has only Dartmouth College which holds the CAE-Research designation. Otherwise, the Southern New Hampshire University (SNHU) offers a handful of cybersecurity programs at multiple levels. At the graduate level they offer a MS in Justice Studies with an optional cybersecurity specialization and a MS in Information Technology – Information Security degree. Additionally, they have a graduate certificate in cybersecurity and a Bachelor's in Information Technology – Information Security. At the junior college level there is an interesting cybersecurity curriculum being taught at Manchester Community College. At Manchester there is a two-year degree program in Cyber Investigations that has a decided forensics focus.

Companies

NH has a modest industrial base for cybersecurity. Some major information security employers in the state are BAE Systems, Bank of America, the State Government of NH, and Liberty Mutual.

Other Notations

Regarding NSF funding, Dartmouth College collects considerable grants (cursory search of awards is well over $2,000,000) from federal funding sources.

NEW JERSEY

New Jersey is a state with a relatively high level of cybersecurity activity. Their cybersecurity posture is built on a solid legal foundation with data breach and cyber-bullying laws with a very involved state government and state police force. Their educational system is robust and they have six CAEs with a variety of academic research centers contributing to theory and practice. NJ does not have the established industrial cybersecurity base that states like North Carolina, Maryland, and California have but New Jersey is positioned as an upcoming tech center with considerable expected growth in sectors with cyber security relevance. Of particular interest is the state's engagement with programs like Cyber Aces and Cyber Patriot that seek to recruit and place young cybersecurity talent and returning military veterans in cybersecurity positions.

State / Policy Activities

New Jersey has a comprehensive data breach notification law with N.J. Stat. § 56:8-163, enacted in 2005/2005. The law is fairly standard although it has a reputation for complexity and differs from many laws in that it requires victims to report breaches to the NJ State Police as opposed to a state consumer agency or government body. New Jersey has a number of cyber related government offices and bodies including a state ISAC, a department of information security with a portal, and a state homeland security & preparedness organization with a cyber-mission. The state police also have an information security unit and other IT related groups working on technology crime and researching means by which crime can more effectively be dealt with through leveraging technological assets. They also appear to have Cyber Aces and Cyber Patriot programs running that seek to educate and develop cyber talent.

New Jersey has a cyber-bullying law on their books and the Governor has been active in promoting cybersecurity as an area of concern. Towards this end, they have the Cyber Foundations initiative which is summarized as "Governor Chris Christie is challenging students from across New Jersey to a statewide competition to identify and develop New Jersey's best talent in cybersecurity and to help them get a solid head start on one of the fastest growing and most lucrative careers. The New Jersey Governor's Cup CyberChallenge will help the nation fill the critical skills gap in cybersecurity."

There is focus on returning veterans and their potential role in filling cybersecurity vacancies... *"New Jersey Gov. Chris Christie has invited service members returning from the Middle East, students and career switchers to join a cyber battle this week for a spot at a community college program with residencies at critical sector companies, state officials told Nextgov."*

Centers / Facilities

New Jersey has only one FFRDC with the Princeton Plasma Physics Laboratory, historically and at present their mission has been to research cutting edge physics and nuclear fusion. Their cybersecurity relevance is nebulous at best. Otherwise the major research and practice centers are located at the state's many educational institutions.

Universities

New Jersey has six NSA CAEs at the following schools: Fairleigh Dickinson University, New Jersey City University, New Jersey Institute of Technology, Princeton, Rutgers, and Stevens Institute of Technology.

Below I've included descriptions of some of the CAEs and their programs.

Rutgers University description from their webpage -- *The Rutgers Center for Information Assurance (RUCIA) is chartered to advance education, foster applied research, and serve as a liaison between Rutgers University and industry and government in the Information Assurance practice and related disciplines. RUCIA aims to establish a national reputation and leadership role in the areas of information assurance, information systems, computer security, systems reliability, data mining and national security. In 2008, RU has been evaluated and certified by the*

Information Assurance Courseware Evaluation (IACE) Program that RU courseware meets all of the elements of the Committee on National Security Systems (CNSS) National Training Standards for Information Systems Security (INFOSEC) Professionals, NSTISSI No. 4011 and System Administrators (SA), CNSSI No. 4013 Entry Level.

Princeton description taken from news article -- *The federal government announced last summer that Princeton will have special status as a hub for cybersecurity research, opening the door to more research such as Lu's, which uses engineering expertise to solve national security problems. Universities with this status are designated a National Center of Academic Excellence in Information Assurance Research. The program is administered by the National Security Agency (NSA) and the Department of Homeland Security (DHS).*

Stevens Institute of Technology, which has a graduate degree program in cybersecurity and for a description of their center see following excerpt from their site -- *The mission of the center is to foster collaboration and act as a catalyst for research, education, and entrepreneurship in information assurance and cybersecurity. Advances in the field require conceptualizing, measuring, modeling, and countering a multitude of rapidly evolving threats. Crucial efforts to meet these challenges include investigation of appropriate theoretical frameworks, novel analysis of existing defense mechanisms, technical innovations, development and deployment of commercial solutions, adoption of suitable policies and standards, and education of systems professionals, managers, policy-makers, and the general population. The center promotes a cohesive undertaking of the above endeavors to maximize their effectiveness and impact.*

The other CAEs all provide similar programs and ultimately NJ has a very robust educational base with a high level of activity in cybersecurity research and education.

Companies

New Jersey is slotted as a major growth state for tech jobs and has established clusters in the financial services and bio-tech industries. At Present, I can't find enormous evidence of cybersecurity firms locating in

NJ but it is likely given their educated workforce, proximity to Wall Street, and government support that they will develop a respectable security base in coming years.

NEW MEXICO

New Mexico has a moderate level of cybersecurity activity. The level of activity is largely built upon the presence of Sandia National Lab and Los Alamos National Lab with a couple of active universities working in the cyber research and education space. The state is among the last in the US to enact any sort of comprehensive data breach protection law, going without such a statue until early 2014. The state has two CAEs and the two aforementioned labs contributing to cyber research initiatives. The Western Cyber Exchange program includes New Mexico and should be further examined for potentially important lessons. Ultimately, New Mexico should not be counted among the "power house" states in our analysis.

State / Policy Activities

Prior to 2014, New Mexico was one of only a handful of states that did not have a comprehensive data breach statute on their books. In early 2014, New Mexico's House passed their first data breach bill.

Regarding New Mexico's data breach bill. Taken from

http://www.naag.org/aftermath-of-the-target-data-breach-state-laws-and-bills.php --

Turning to New Mexico, its House passed H.B. 224 on Feb. 17, a bill which would require any person owning, maintaining or possessing the personally identifiable information of a state resident to notify affected individuals within 10 days of discovering a breach and also notify the state attorney general within 10 business days if more than 50 residents were affected. The bill also contains provisions for credit card breaches and would require companies to implement and maintain reasonable security and data disposal procedures. The bill would give the state attorney general authority to seek injunctive relief and recovery of actual damages, as well as a civil penalty of up to $150,000 for failure to notify.

NM has an ISAC as part of the compulsory national strategy and they have state-level homeland security and emergency management office. The state IT department publishes their security policies which appear fairly standard. I see no major efforts to promote user awareness or public education on cyber and see little mention of large scale training and preparation for state-level cyber response.

Centers / Facilities

NM is home to two major cybersecurity research centers with Sandia National Laboratory and the famous Los Alamos National Laboratory. Sandia has a broad cybersecurity mission that includes SCADA security, analytics, education, and other work that is related to their historical mission of protecting the US nuclear arsenal's safety mechanisms.

They also host the Center for Cyber Defenders, which is an educational program for qualified students to learn practical cybersecurity skills. Taken from their website -- *The Center for Cyber Defenders Program gives computer science students practical experience directed towards understanding computer systems, network operations, and information protection. The mentors and staff of the Cyber Defender program have developed a unique environment that challenges students with cutting edge research projects, while supplying multiple levels of new skills for students with varied computer backgrounds. It also provides students with a legitimate venue for performing experiments on attacking and defending computer systems with proper guidance and protective measures in place.*

Los Alamos has a cybersecurity department with the following mission statement -- *Our focus is to provide nationally recognized leadership in information security and networking science that predicts and solves critical problems in the cyber domain using novel practical solutions. Our work includes national security work, industrial partnerships, and the open research featured on this site. They have specialized projects ongoing in areas like insider threat detection, energy grid security, quantum cryptography, and malware classification.*

The Western Cyber Exchange, a new public-private collaboration supported by DHS and MITRE is taking shape and NM is one of the states included. This is a description taken from a Dark Reading article -- *The WCX includes the states of Colorado, New Mexico, and Wyoming with the WCX Laboratories in Colorado Springs. WCX has been promoting a new, grassroots* approach to collective cybersecurity since 2010. The WCX is the first organization of its kind a public/private partnership designed to share information related to ever-increasing cybersecurity threats, support workforce development through education and training programs, and the development of new technology through research and development programs. WCX is a non-profit, member organization which includes members from utilities, the defense industrial base, education, manufacturing, the IT sector, and finance. For this threat exchange demonstration, WCX was supported by Imprimis Inc., an advanced engineering and technology firm and a founding member of WCX.

Universities

There are two NSA CAEs located in New Mexico. There is one at the University of New Mexico's Center for Information Assurance Research and Education. They have a SFS program and boast partnerships with the FBI's regional computer forensics lab (RCFL) and the Cyber Defenders initiative at Sandia National Labs.

The second CAE is located at New Mexico Tech, a small school specializing in science in technology. A description of their program is taken from their site's home page -- *The expertise in the Information Assurance (IA) in the Computer Science & Engineering Department at New Mexico Tech provides a unique set of capabilities to address the issues related to security and assurance of information systems. This program has been established to fulfill a strong need for research that coordinates and exploits the fusion among the diverse set of technical expertise of the school as well as the university to solve the multidimensional problems of information assurance.*

Companies

New Mexico has a couple of industrial clusters with some relevance to cybersecurity but lacks the deep tech industry presence seen in California, North Carolina and Washington. The presence of Kirtland AFB and a number of national labs bring in many Aerospace companies like

Honeywell and Lockheed. There is some tech involvement (small Intel plant, etc.) but nothing like the involvement seen in classic high-tech areas.

NEW YORK

New York is the financial/banking nerve center of the US economy with international ramifications. New York is following close behind California in the legislative aspect of cyber regulations. Their focus is on financial and business repercussions of cyber security and the impact on the broad implications to national and international financial systems. New York State emphasizes terrorism and natural disasters above cyber security which is the 10th item on their list of statewide strategies.

State / Policy Activities

Cybersecurity policy and political activities happen on the State and NY City levels. In 2013 Governor Cuomo established a Cyber Security Advisory Board to guide state government on developments in cyber security and make recommendations for protecting the state's critical infrastructure and information systems. New York's governor is working to position New York as a leader in cybersecurity to attract the growing industry of cyber-related business to the state. Focus on the banking industry is a major strategy and NYS Department of Financial Services has "'required' 200 banks to assess cyber policies and processes." Proposed state legislation would make New York the first state to legislate virtual currency and addressing the BitLicense regime.

NYS Homeland Security Strategy2014-16's 10 point goal includes enhanced cyber security capabilities as the 10th point. There is little integration of the cyber component to other relevant goals such as maintenance and protection of critical infrastructure. Interruption of the New York economy has national and international ramifications and considerable emphasis on interruptions through physical terrorism and weather conditions dominate strategic thinking.

New York hosts a variety of cybersecurity conferences. The 17th New York State Cybersecurity Conference and 9th Annual Symposium on Information Assurance had over 1100 attendees. Smaller conferences, New

York Metro Joint Cyber Security Conference, Western New York Cyber Security Conference and

New York's senator has presented new legislation in the Cyber Information Sharing Tax Credit Act which will incentive business communities across sectors to join" the Information Sharing and Analysis Centers (ISACs), generating the perception that NYS is leading the call for cyber security regulations.

Centers / Facilities

Multi-State Information Sharing & Analysis Center

The mission of the MS-ISAC is to improve the overall cyber security posture of state, local, tribal and territorial governments. Collaboration and information sharing among members, private sector partners and the U.S. Department of Homeland Security are the keys to success. Executive Committee representatives come from 11 states across the nation.

Public-Private Working Group (PPWG) links NY and NJ

Center for Internet Security (501 c3)

Focuses on enhancing the cyber security readiness and response of public and private sector entities, with a commitment to excellence through collaboration. Trusted Purchasing Alliance serves state, local, territorial and tribal governments and related not-for-profit entities in achieving a greater cyber security posture through trusted expert guidance and cost-effective procurement.

Integrated Intelligence Center

Facilitates trusted relationships with government and private sector entities to develop and disseminate comprehensive, coordinated intelligence products that help improve the security posture of all partners.

CIS Security Benchmarks

Develops and distributes consensus-based and internationally recognized solutions that help organizations improve their cyber security and compliance posture.

NYS Forum

A non-profit, sponsors the Cyber Security Conference/IA Conference for government agencies and organizations.

Universities

New York has eight Centers for Academic Excellence:

- Erie Community College
- Mercy College
- Pace University
- Polytechnic University
- Rochester Institute of Technology
- State University of New York – Buffalo
- Syracuse University
- US Military Academy, West Point

The New York State University system (SUNY) and City University system of New York, (CUNY) provide cybersecurity degrees at multiple locations throughout their extensive networks., as does the There are additional private schools, NY Institute of Technology (NYIT) and extensions of DeVry and ITT

Companies

- Cyber Security Auditors & ADM
- Cybersecurity Integrators, Inc.
- Cyber Security Institute, Inc.
- Cyber Communications & NY Security

- Cyber Diligence, Inc.
- Promia Cyber Securities, Inc.
- Wilson, Elser, Moskowitz, Edelman & Dicker LLP
- Grassi & Co
- Marcum LLP
- ISecure

There is an extensive list of accounting, consulting and law firms focused on the growing sector of cyber security related business.

Other Notations

1) Cyber Security Advisory Board Members: Richard Clark, Shawn Henry, Will Pelgrin, Phil Reitinger, Howard Schmidt.

2) Additional educational institutions offering security courses as part of their degree:
   - http://education-portal.com/computer_information_systems_degrees_in_new_york.html Private Sector

3) NY State's 2014-16 Homeland Security Strategy.
   - http://www.dhses.ny.gov/media/documents/NYS-Homeland-Security-Strategy.pdf

4) NYS focus is the financial and legal industries.
   - http://www.banktech.com/compliance/state-governments-and-the-future-of-cyber-security-regulation/d/d-id/1279216

NORTH CAROLINA

Simply put, North Carolina is one of the cybersecurity "hot beds." They have a very large and very active research agenda supported by a highly collaborative network of universities, companies, and government bodies. NC was an early adopter of the research park model and has attracted lots of high technology companies and research ventures with parks like the famous Research Triangle. Research parks were first created at Stanford and they seek to facilitate technology transfer, advanced research, and scientific innovation through the co-location of university and private industry researchers. There are research centers working on the majority of key cybersecurity topics with special attention being paid to big data, high performance computing, electric grid security, and embedded systems security. More than a dozen large high technology companies have a presence in the state including Cisco, SAS, Red Hat, and Verizon. The state's many collaborative research projects that span academia and industry attract fairly enormous funding from the NSF, DOD, and Intelligence Community. NC cyber research projects include a $60 million funding grant from the NSA and more than 20 currently active NSF cybersecurity grant awards that exceed $500,000. The state has a very unique model that is more collaborative than really any other state I've analyzed and merits further examination regarding the research park organization model.

State / Policy Activities

Taken from website article linked below -- *As of October 1, 2009, entities doing business in North Carolina will be required to both provide more detailed data breach notices to individuals and be more forthcoming with the state's attorney general. North Carolina Senate Bill 1017 ("SB 1017"), signed by Governor Bev Perdue on July 27, 2009, amends North Carolina's data breach notification law in two significant ways. First, SB 1017 requires notice to the attorney general anytime a business notifies North Carolina residents of a breach. Previously, such notice had been required only for breaches affecting more than 1,000 people. Second, notices to individuals affected by a breach will now be required to include a telephone number for the business providing the notice; toll-free numbers and addresses for the national credit reporting agencies; and toll-free numbers, addresses and web site addresses for the Federal Trade Commission and the North Carolina Attorney General's Office along with a statement that individuals can learn about preventing identity theft from these sources. These new requirements build on top of existing mandates to (1) describe the incident, the type(s) of personal information unlawfully obtained and the actions being taken to prevent further unauthorized access; (2) provide a telephone number that the recipient may call for further information and assistance; and (3) advise affected individuals to remain vigilant by reviewing account statements and monitoring free credit reports.*

http://privacylaw.proskauer.com/2009/07/articles/security-breach-notification-l/showme-state-finally-shows-its-residents-a-data-breach-notification-law-other-states-tx-nc-me-make-changes/

NC DOJ provides best practice information to residents through alerts and news articles on their webpage. North Carolina has created a cyber-information sharing and analysis center that is part of the larger Multi-State ISAC. The NC-ISAC mission is described here taken from their website... *The mission of the NC-ISAC, consistent with the objectives of the National Strategy to Secure Cyberspace, is to provide a common mechanism for raising the level of cyber security readiness and response in state and local governments. The NC-ISAC provides a central resource for gathering information on cyber threats to critical infrastructure from state agencies and providing two-way sharing of information between and among the state agencies and with local government where permissible.*

NC has an office of Enterprise Security & Risk Management that provides state information security policies and procedures, awareness and training services, threat response, and secure IT procurement directives as part of the NC CIO's and CISO's responsibilities. The NC National Guard is being utilized for state cyber exercises as an FCW.com article notes...*N.C. Guard's Joint Cyber Defense Team along with 300 Soldiers, Airmen and civilians from 35 states and territories, participated in Cyber Shield this spring. The exercise was designed to challenge teams with real-world scenarios where their networks were maliciously attacked again and again.*

Centers / Facilities

NC has the very famous "Research Triangle" which describes an area in central NC where there is an enormous concentration of universities, tech companies, and research centers. The name comes largely from the Research Triangle Park facility which is one of the largest research parks in the US. Built in 1959, it hosts nearly 200 companies, multiple university research centers, and non-profits. The park's tenants employ more than 50,000 people and 100,000 contractors, many of which work in tech companies with security relevance. The research park model has proven attractive in NC and there are at least three other smaller research parks in the state. The park's security relevant tenants are as follows: IBM, Cisco, NetApp, Red Hat, EMC, GE, Lenovo, Qualcomm, Sony Ericsson, and Verizon and others. The park is managed by a non-profit organization now called Research Triangle International (RTI) which also engages in cyber research.

From the RTI website's cybersecurity page...*RTI is part of the Institute for Homeland Security Solutions (IHSS), a collaborative initiative between RTI, Duke University, the University of North Carolina at Chapel Hill, and the North Carolina Military Foundation. IHSS is a research consortium that conducts applied research in the social and behavioral sciences to address a wide range of homeland security challenges.*

North Carolina also hosts the SE branch of the Defense Department's Army Research Laboratory but it does not have any national labs or FFRDCs headquartered in-state. There are also numerous research facilities that operate out of the state's many universities and their research parks. Many of these organizations are described in the section below.

Universities

North Carolina has a pretty massive educational footprint that includes four-year private and public schools as well as community colleges. The programs and schools listed below are by no means exhaustive but instead represent the "heavy hitters" in regards to cyber/IT research and education.

There are four NSA CAEs located in North Carolina at UNC-Charlotte, East Carolina University, NC State University, and North Carolina A&T State University. These schools provide instruction at multiple levels in information security topics.

The University of NC system is enormous and many of the schools offer cyber related curriculum and courses. Below, there is a screen shot of the UNC's core competencies for defense that are related to cybersecurity.

Analytics, Computing, Cybersecurity

"Big data" analytics, mining, visualization, high performance computing, modeling & simulation wireless communication, cyber, virtual training, remote sensing & image analysis, GIS terrain modeling & data integration

- UNC Charlotte Visualization Center
- NC State Laboratory for Analytic Science, Institute for Advanced Analytics
- Renaissance Computing Institute
- UNC Charlotte Center for Configuration Analytics and Automation, Cyber Defense and Network Assurability Center
- NC A&T Visualization Center, Center for Cyber Defense
- NC State Computer Science, Digital Games Research Center
- UNC Chapel Hill Computer Science, Project Silver
- UNC Chapel Hill Geography, City & Regional Planning, Anthropology
- NCCU Wireless Communication, Physics / Mathematics, NASA URC

The State is also home to Duke University which has historically been very active in legal studies, terrorism, privacy, and national security and its researchers collaborate with the many companies and schools in the state. Duke partners with the aforementioned RTI to operate an interdisciplinary research center devoted to homeland security and defense.

North Carolina Agricultural & Technical University is one of the CAE certified schools and has a number of cyber projects ongoing. For example, see this description taken from their website -- *The Center for Advanced Studies in Identity Sciences (CASIS) is performing research in the areas of advanced biometrics and cyber identity protection & privacy. CASIS is funded by grants from the Army Research Laboratory, the National Science Foundation, and the National Nuclear Security Administration. North Carolina A&T State University and Guilford Technical Community College (GTCC) have launched an independent and joint research partnership in cyber security at N.C. A&T's Center for Advanced Studies in Identity Sciences (CASIS) and the Center for Cyber Defense (C2D). The Center for Cyber Defense (C2D) is performing research in cyber security. It has been designated as a National Center of Academic Excellence in Information Assurance Education by the National Security Agency and the Department of Homeland Security. C2D is funded by grants from the National Science Foundation, the Department of Education, and the National Nuclear Security Administration. Also home to the Center for Cyber Defense.*

North Carolina State University is also quite active in the cyber research space. North Carolina State University is one of four schools nationwide that's been awarded $2.5 million in grant funds from the U.S. National Security Agency (NSA) to do research work on the design/analysis of trusted systems. Additionally, NC State has been awarded a $60.75 million grant from the NSA to form the Laboratory for Analytic Sciences in a Centennial Campus building that will do research on big data (http://www.newsobserver.com/2013/08/15/3109412_nc-state-teams-up-with-nsa-on.html?rh=1). Centennial Campus is also home to the FREEDM Systems Center, one of the latest Gen-III Engineering Research Centers (ERC) established by the National Science Foundation in 2008 to develop technology to integrate the nation's power grid with renewable electrical energy technologies. NC State host multiple laboratories and research centers/groups focusing on issues related to security (big data, embedded systems, cloud computing et al.) Additionally, they are helping to develop what are termed NSA "lablets" which are interesting concept that blends intelligence work and classified research on select campuses.

Methodist University has cyber degree minors focusing on network security and digital forensics.

Companies

The companies have been listed above in earlier sections. The state has a broad cybersecurity research agenda with groups doing research in virtually all the standard areas. There are a number of economic factors that seem to differentiate some of NC's specializations. Principally, NC has one of the highest concentrations of life sciences companies and thus there is a large interest in bio-informatics, healthcare IT security and patient data security. There are numerous bio-tech firms as well as a large DuPont chemical facility that likely contribute to some of the state's focus on protecting IP and securing data. NC is also home to Duke Energy which is absolutely one of the largest energy utilities in America and thus there's considerable focus on grid security, next-gen cyber physical systems, and embedded systems security. There is also huge interest and activity in big data and cloud computing. NC State is the alma mater of the founders of the software and analytics giant SAS and they maintain a large presence in the state.

See earlier sections for further detail.

Other Notations

A cursory search of the NSF award list has 22 currently active cybersecurity grants for schools in NC that exceed $500,000. Also, there is multi-million dollar funding from the Pentagon and Intelligence Community. In essence, they get that money.

NORTH DAKOTA

North Dakota's cybersecurity efforts and capabilities are quite limited. They have no NSA Centers of Academic Excellence, their universities offering very little in the way of security curricula, and they lack major facilities and funding devoted to information security practice, theory, and study.

State / Policy Activities

North Dakota has a fairly standard data breach notification law on their books that was last updated in 2013 to include a person's health insurance information. They also have a cyber-bullying law in place as of 2013. The state government does have an office of IT Security and there is a state CISO. The ND state government's IT Security department maintains a webpage with best practices, alerts, and other guidance but it appears to be only infrequently updated. There exists a ND state government office focusing on homeland security and emergency services but there appears to be limited focus on cyber planning or exercises. My internet searching has not located any evidence of high-level state government working groups, policy advisers, or coordinated exercises focusing on information security. The state is part of a Multi-State ISAC through DHS but other coordinating or leadership activities appear scarce.

Centers / Facilities

My internet research has turned up no evidence of private, public, or pseudo-public institutions or groups engaged in specialized cybersecurity research or practice.

Universities

The cybersecurity offerings at the university level in ND are extremely limited. I can evidence of one brick and mortar cybersecurity degree program at an institution called Rasmussen College in Fargo/Bismarck,

ND. There are no NSA CAEs located in the state and there exists only one brick and mortar digital forensics program but it is located the community college level.

Companies

Outside of the ubiquitous presence of Military Industrial Complex companies that do cybersecurity contracting there appears to be little commercial focus on cybersecurity in ND. I found job postings for SAIC that seem to be located in ND but other evidence was not easily located.

Other Notations

Basically, ND does not appear to be a major cybersecurity state.

Guiding Questions

1) Legislation at the state level in the area of cybersecurity.
    a. Has a data breach law, updated 2013 to include health information and health insurance information. Requires notification, if exceeding 250k or 500k in some circumstances email, news, or a website announcement are sufficient means of notification.
    b. North Dakota has a cybersecurity awareness month in October, as of 2013.
    c. Has a cyber-bullying law in place
    d. ND government has an IT security department, ND has a CISO.
        i. Website offers best practices, guidance, tips, but not updated since 2013
    e. Can't find much on working groups, planning, or other exercises.

f. Has a State Department of HS/ES… very little cyber focus though

g. Are part of a MS-ISAC

2) Centers of cybersecurity research/practice.

   a. No centers of excellence, no SFS programs

   b. Rasmussen College in Fargo/Bismarck has bachelor's and associate degrees

   c. Devry

   d. Only one place offering Forensics specialization at Southwestern Community College

3) Technical/analytical cybersecurity facilities in the state.

   a. Basically nothing

4) What are the state's cybersecurity main research/practice focus(es).

   a. Nothing

5) What funding do they have from the funding agencies (NSF, etc.).

   a. Nothing

OHIO

Generally speaking, Ohio has a moderate level of cybersecurity activity. They do have the basic state government resources and oversight expected from a state of its size and they are engaging in some state directed cybersecurity research, development, and improvement efforts. Ohio has four centers of excellence and a handful of other four year schools providing cybersecurity education. Their educational posture is solid but lacks the breadth or size of states like Texas, North Carolina, or California. The state does have a number of large research universities like Ohio State and Cincinnati working on information security. The state has a large quantity of cybersecurity education being delivered through the two-year community college system. Ohio appears to have a relatively high number of associate degree or other two-year programs oriented towards cybersecurity. The cybersecurity companies and research facilities are not particularly large in either size or number. In conclusion, it would appear that Ohio lies somewhere in the *middle of the pack* when it comes to cybersecurity.

State / Policy Activities

Ohio has a fairly standard data breach notification law and they do have both a CISO and a Chief Privacy Officer for the state. The state does maintain a centralized privacy and security webpage to inform citizens about cybersecurity issues and to offer best practices guidelines for its residents. The level of activity in the state appears to be moderate although past cybersecurity incidents (Anonymous hacking the state's web portal) seem to be pushing the state forward on cybersecurity. The state is providing funding for studying information security but not at the levels seen in other states like California or Delaware.

Centers / Facilities

In February 2014 Ohio initiated the Columbus Collaboratory...Taken from http://development.ohio.gov/files/media/pressrelease/2.12.14

The project establishes a central location where companies can work together and develop tools to perform advanced analytics and improve cybersecurity. The Ohio Third Frontier Commission approved $5 million to support the Columbus Collaboratory, a multiple industry partnership to make Ohio a leader in advanced analytics and cybersecurity. The Columbus Collaboratory will create 100 new jobs over the next five years. A $20 million investment will come from American Electric Power, Battelle, Cardinal Health, Huntington Bank, L Brands, Nationwide and OhioHealth.

Riverside Research

Riverside Research is an independent, not-for-profit organization chartered to advance scientific research in the public interest and in support of the United States government. Comprised of leading engineering, technology, and operations experts, we strive to consistently deliver trusted, mission-focused solutions in: bio-medical, cyber, and ISR.

Battelle Memorial

Battelle Memorial Institute is headquartered in Columbus. The Institute is heavily involved in the management of the US National Lab system overseeing labs like PNNL and LLNL.

Universities

Ohio has four NSA Centers of Academic Excellence (Air Force Institute of Technology, Ohio State University, Owens Community College and Sinclair Community College).

University of Dayton offers some information security options with the MBA program summed up in this description taken from their site... *The*

University of Dayton's Masters in Business Administration (MBA) program and the Riverside Research are offering students the unique opportunity to take a three-course sequence in cyber security management, resulting in a certificate or MBA concentration. This credential qualifies students to support the government and industry through addressing domain specific requirements and preparing candidates for three highly sought after DoD 8570 Certifications: (ISC)2 Certification & Accreditation Professional (CAP), CompTIA's Network+ and Security+. In one year, qualified students are able to obtain three DoD 8570 certifications and complete approximately one third of the course requirements toward their MBA.

The University of Cincinnati's College of Engineering and Applied Science has recently had their electrical engineering program certified as a center of excellence in cyber operations for 2014-2019.

There are efforts ongoing at Miami University AKA Miami of Ohio to bolster their information security research and education capabilities. They have recently opened a new cyber lab described on their site as...*The Fortinet CyberSecurity Laboratory, said Thomas J. LeBlanc, UM's executive vice president and provost, "will propel the college's Department of Electrical and Computer Engineering to the forefront of research and education in cybersecurity."*

Case Western University and Cleveland State University have both added new hands-on cybersecurity education options. Taken from

http://engineering.case.edu/cyber-security-courses

Come fall, students at Case Western Reserve University and Cleveland State University will begin hacking computers—for credit. Each university is offering the first of three courses in a new curriculum in which engineering and computer science students will learn how to break into — and then protect — hardware, software and data. The goal is for students to understand how they can then protect their own, or their employer's, computers from viruses, phishing attacks, so-called Trojan horses and other cyber-attacks.

Wright State University is offering the first Master's degree in cybersecurity in Ohio as of 2012.

There are many community colleges offering cybersecurity degree programs or certificates with a brief subset mentioned below.

Belmont College...*The 2-year Associate of Applied Science, Information Technology - Cyber Security and Computer Forensics program is Belmont College's newest Information Technology degree designed to propel you into an entry-level position in network security.*

Stark State College...*The cyber security and computer forensics technology program covers areas that are identified in the Emergency Preparedness and Response, Information Analysis and Infrastructure Protection divisions of the Department of Homeland Security.*

Companies

- Verizon
- Stealth Entry
- Jurinovv LTD
- Booz Allen Hamilton
- ABB
- JP Morgan Chase
- Northrup Grumman
- GE
- IBM
- Battelle
- Lunarline, Inc.

OKLAHOMA

State / Policy Activities

Oklahoma has a well-integrated inter agency Cyber Security Group (CSG) with Special Interests Groups (SIG) meeting quarterly since 2004. Designed to address the gaps in policy, training, administration and education, the state's cyber stance has matured and continues to utilize a systemic approach to hone cyber awareness across agencies, industry clusters and a strong commitment to develop their citizens to qualify for cybersecurity positions. Oklahoma maintains a progressive stance in terms of cyber security education, research and a strong integration with workforce development through their two year schools.

Centers / Facilities

Oklahoma clearly defined their IT/Cybersecurity policies and procedures in 2003 with updates to their on-line manual in 2011. The state meetings regularly with their agencies and conducts quarterly meetings, table exercises and integrates their activities with the OK Homeland Security Department. The state has made

http://www.ok.gov/OSF/documents/StateOfOklahomaInfoSecPPG_osf_12012008.pdf

The State participated in the NASCIO social media workgroup and is one of a score of States using Facebook to update citizens with government activities.

Laws: 21-1951.

This act shall be known and may be cited as the "Oklahoma Computer Crimes Act". Initiated 1984 with updates related to cyber crimes, initially crimes involved with computers.

http://www.forwardedge2.com/pdf/OK-laws.pdf;

penalties ran from $5,000 to $100,000 in penalties with jail time.

24 Okla. Stat. § 161 et seq. passed in 2008 lays out guidelines for security breech notification within Oklahoma.

Universities

Oklahoma has six Centers for Academic Excellence and Research. Four are two year schools: Francis Tuttle Technology School, Oklahoma City Community College, Oklahoma Department of Career & Technology and Rose State College. Oklahoma State University and University of Tulsa are the four year CAE. Oklahoma's 2004 NSF $3 million grant built a strong 2 year/4 year educational network. In 2007 an additional $2.7 million developed a deeper connection to workforce development.[1] Within the 29 technology centers at 58 campus sites, a range of courses, including networking through higher level certification courses at the CAE-R 2Y are available.

Companies

Center for Telecommunications and Network Security at Oklahoma State University. CTANS was established in 2002 to serve as the focal point for education and research for information assurance in the OSU system and is connected to a CAE-R. The state is running the Oklahoma's Cyber Command.

Oklahoma is a member of the Cyber Security Education Consortium "a cohesive partnership of community colleges and career and technology centers in Arkansas, Colorado, Kansas, Louisiana, Missouri, Tennessee and Texas and the University of Tulsa, which serves as the principal training entity and mentor to the two-year institutions."[2] Security Operations

---

[1] http://www.okcareertech.org/news/press-releases/2009/cyber-security-education-consortium-awarded-2.7-million-grant-to-expand-workforce
[2] http://www.okcareertech.org/about/initiatives/cyber-security

Center, is connected to the FBI and has a staff of 3. It appears to be receiving threat notification from the feds.

Armed Forces Communication and Electronics Association, AFCEA, has an active presence in Oklahoma and has conducted an annual conference for ten years.

Other Notations

1) Laws:
   http://www.irongeek.com/i.php?page=computerlaws/state-hacking-laws

2) http://www.ncsl.org/programs/lis/CIP/hacklaw.htm
   http://www.onlinesecurity.com/forum/article46.php
   http://law.justia.com/
   http://w2.eff.org/Net_culture/Hackers/comp_crime_laws_by_state.l ist

3) http://www.nascio.org/awards/nominations/2009/2009OK9-2009%20Awards%20-%20Cyber%20Security%20Group.pdf

4) Early start on education in 2004.
   http://www.occc.edu/News/Archive-2004/CyberSecurity.html

5) General:
   http://www.nascio.org/publications/documents/NASCIO_FirstNet_June2014_FINAL.pdf

6) Technology centers: http://www.okcareertech.org/technology-centers

7) Good source of what is the latest:
   http://www.thecyberwire.com/events.html

8) Social Media work group:
   https://www.ok.gov/cio/documents/FacebookTOSMediaRelease01112011.pdf

OREGON

Oregon has a relatively high level of cybersecurity activity, especially for a state of its relative size and population. Oregon has the major data breach laws and an active state government that participates in exercises and is engaged in new law-making and funding for cybersecurity. The state does not have major cybersecurity relevant national labs or FFRDCs but has a number of organizations and institutions engaging in IA research both privately and publically. The educational component is relatively small but there appears to be active engagement and research going on at schools like Portland State, Univ. of Oregon, and Oregon State University as well as a number of options for two-year education. The state also has a respectable tech and software industry base making security products, solutions, and hardware. In general, Oregon is likely to be regarded as a state with upper medium to high levels of cybersecurity activity.

State / Policy Activities

Oregon has a standard data breach notification law on their books that was enacted in 2007 (§ 646A.604). Additionally they have the Oregon Identity Theft Protection Act

http://www.cbs.state.or.us/dfcs/id_theft.html

and there's talk of proposing digital privacy legislation in the next year. The state government offers a fairly standard website for enterprise security and information security resources, providing basic guidance, best practices, and news related to information security. The sites are located at

http://www.oregon.gov/DAS/CIO/ISRC/pages/index.aspx
http://www.oregon.gov/DAS/CIO/ESO/pages/secplan.aspx

Also, Oregon participated in the Department of Homeland Security's CyberStorm IV exercises. The purpose of the event is described as follows...*State exercises are two-day tabletop events where representatives from a variety of state departments and agencies assess their cyber response plans. They identify and simulate how to engage elements across state governance, as well as* cybersecurity partners such as law enforcement entities and the private sector. Throughout the event, participants can validate policies, plans, and procedures that enable response, recovery, and continuity of operations. Players, planners, and observers represent a variety of positions, including technical and non-technical staff, emergency managers, public affairs representatives, and leadership. Through CS IV, DHS designed, conducted, and evaluated exercises for seven states including: Maine, Oregon, Washington, Idaho, Missouri, Mississippi, and Nevada.

http://www.dhs.gov/cyber-storm-securing-cyber-space

Oregon has taken efforts to extend information security learning down to elementary and high school level education...*The Education Information Security Council (EISC) is responsible for setting the vision, direction, and best practices regarding information security across all levels of preK-12 education institutions in Oregon. This includes strategic planning, policy development, and identification and pursuit of opportunities to collaborate on information security initiatives.*

http://www.ode.state.or.us/search/page/?id=3558

At the state funding level there is interest in building a cybersecurity center for excellence...*Oregon tech leaders have refined their plans for a new, state-sponsored "Center for Cyber Excellence" and have cut their request for legislative funding by more than half. They're now seeking $2.5 million over two years to hire an executive director and kick off the project. The project aims to create a pipeline of skilled workers from Oregon universities to go to work in cyber security, support research in the field and build cyber awareness at businesses – and even in elementary and high schools.*

http://www.govtech.com/budget-finance/Oregon-Tech-Leaders-will-Seek-25-million-for-Center-for-Cyber-Excellence.html

Centers / Facilities

Many of the state's academics and colleges have participated in study groups and organizations, for example...*The Regional Alliance for Infrastructure and Network Security (RAINS) is a non-profit, private/public* partnership formed to accelerate the development and deployment of innovative technology for homeland security. PSU students perform research and development on a network infrastructure designed to allow first-responders to communicate securely about emergency situations.

http://www.pdx.edu/news/nsa-designates-portland-state-quotcenter-academic-excellence-information-assurance-educationquot

At Oregon State University they are building partnerships for cybersecurity research in applied fields like energy. For example... *The Energy Sector Security Consortium (EnergySec) and Oregon State University's Open Source Lab (OSUOSL) announced today that they will partner to perform strategic research on the current use of open source software in the energy sector, especially as it relates to computer security. OSUOSL will perform case studies looking at leading and influential organizations or projects, the tools they use and the challenges these groups have faced in adopting open source software.*

http://www.energysec.org/press-release/energy-sector-security-consortium-and-the-oregon-state-university-open-source-lab-partner-to-establish-effective-and-inclusive-collaboration-and-governance-models/ and http://osuosl.org/

At University of Oregon there are a couple of ongoing research partnerships and academic centers performing cybersecurity research, publishing, and tool building. Firstly there is OSIRIS, and below that there is the Network & Security Research Lab... *The Oregon Systems Infrastructure Research and Information Security (OSIRIS) Laboratory is a part of the Department of Computer and Information Science at the University of Oregon. Founded by Professor Kevin Butler in the Fall of 2010, the OSIRIS Lab's mission is to discover new research methodologies, technologies, and systems that address timely and important issues in securing computer systems and networks. The scope of our work ranges from individual embedded systems to national-scale infrastructure, and from theoretical models to deployed hardware. We pursue collaborative and multidisciplinary research, and our work has appeared in the top journals, conferences, and workshops in security.*

http://osiris.cs.uoregon.edu/

Network & Security Research Laboratory at University of Oregon. *Networking research and technologies have fundamentally changed people's life, and will continue to do so, probably in more unexpected ways than ever thought. We actively research how to make networking work better and secure, with a focus on topics related to the Internet. We seek cutting-edge solutions that are not only thought-provoking in a lab environment, but also feasible and deployable in the real world. You may click on our research link to your left to view some of our ongoing research projects. Our lab was established after Prof. Jun Li joined U of O in Fall, 2002. We have graduate and undergraduate student researchers, visiting students and scholars, and collaborators from both industry and academia all over the world, closely working together on research topics that we believe to be useful to the society. Our research is mainly supported by USA National Science Foundation.*

http://netsec.cs.uoregon.edu/

Regarding national labs and FFRDCs, Oregon has only one national lab (National Energy Technology Laboratory) with some peripheral relevance to cybersecurity research. The lab's description is as follows...*NETL, with three primary locations in Albany, OR, Morgantown, WV, and Pittsburgh, PA, is the only national laboratory owned and operated by the United States Department of Energy. Its mission is to strengthen our nation's security, to improve our nation's environment, and to advance energy options that fuel our nation's economy. To complement NETL's mission, ORISE educational programs help to ensure that NETL has a robust supply of scientists and engineers to meet its future science and technology needs.*

http://netl.doe.gov/about

Universities

The only Center of Academic Excellence in Oregon is located at Portland State University (PSU). The National Security Agency (NSA) designated Portland State University as a Center of Academic Excellence in Information Assurance Education beginning in 2003. The designation award is described in the following excerpt from a news article...*NSA granted this year's designations following a rigorous review of university applications against published criteria based on training standards established by the National Security Telecommunications and Information Systems Security Committee (NSTISSC). Formal presentations will be made June 3, 2003, in Washington, D.C., at the 2003 Colloquium for Information Systems Security Education. PSU is the only university in Oregon or Washington to be recognized, and one of approximately 50 in the United States.*

http://www.pdx.edu/news/nsa-designates-portland-state-quotcenter-academic-excellence-information-assurance-educationquot

PSU also has created a unique digital forensics laboratory with the Laboratory for Digital Forensics and Security Research in the College of Engineering and Computer Science.

There course offerings in cybersecurity are summarized on the department's site as...*courses at PSU include Cryptography, Introduction to Computer Security, Malicious Code and Forensics (computer viruses), Introduction to Computer Forensics, Network Management and Security and others. Information about these courses can be found at www.cs.pdx.edu. Portland State's program, a master's in computer science with a concentration in security, is the only one to be certified in Oregon or Washington and one of only a few nationally.* They have four faculty members specializing in security topics like network security, malware analysis and cryptography.

At the two-year community college level there are additional educational opportunities for students looking for cybersecurity training.

MHCC is the one of the few community colleges in Oregon offering an AAS in CyberSecurity & Networking.

http://www.occ-sec.com/

Additionally, Portland Community College offers an associate's degree in health informatics and two cybersecurity certificates and Chemeketa Community College offers a certificate in network management and systems security.

http://www.oregonlive.com/portland/index.ssf/2013/04/mt_hood_community_college_resp.html

Companies

Oregon has a fairly robust IT and software industry and unsurprisingly many of those companies have entered into the security business. According to an OSU news article "there are about 20 companies in Oregon doing computer security-related work, one of the largest concentrations of cyber-security industry experts in the nation."

http://oregonstate.edu/ua/ncs/archives/2002/aug/oregon-front-lines-fighting-cyber-terrorism

Specifically, some of those companies includes Flir Systems, ID Experts, EID Passport, Kryptiq and Tripwire. As well as, Mentor Graphics and Intel – working with its McAfee subsidiary – are developing hardware-based technologies to guard against online snooping.

Funding Opportunities

Source of Funding: Federal support, industry funding and National Security Foundation (NSF), Intel, Google, MIT Lincoln Labs, Battelle and ARO. Total research funding to date is about $8.49 million.

Resources for Start-ups

Approximately $3.0 million in initial funding has been budgeted to meet the needs of the tasks defined above. This includes full stand-up and staffing of the Program Management Office and provisioning the initial resources until the next budget cycle. Approximately $2.3 million per year is needed in the budget to sustain the program. The bulk of these funds are for personnel to set in place the collaborative initiatives needed to create a Centre for Cyber Excellence in Oregon. Included in this cost is approximately $150k to establish the office including furniture, modifications to the space, office equipment and IT infrastructure.

The state encourages start-ups to collaborate with sponsors through research centres. Oregon State University researchers already work for or with industry to develop new technologies and solutions where their expertise specifically addresses company needs. The Centre for Cyber Excellence (COE) provides a new vehicle to grow and expand local research partnerships through the development of widely applicable innovative solutions, and delivering a prepared and engaged workforce. The COE makes it a priority to support the cyber-security research needs of Oregon based companies and industries. These partnerships will drive economic growth by creating new solutions to emerging problems and supply an educated workforce ready to hit the ground running. Leveraging the local knowledge and contact, the COE can provide a practical framework to ease the challenges of public-private partnerships.

Other Notations

The State of Oregon

A unique opportunity exists in the Oregon cyber-security community today; by virtue of how the state has developed over the years and with consideration for the immense investment by the business community. Oregon has a unique opportunity to collaboratively create the next generation, cyber-savvy workforce. An Educational Needs Assessment for the Engineering Technology Industry Council" corroborated by the Technology Association of Oregon (TAO) sponsored survey of employers, Oregon needs to rapidly increase the number of cyber-savvy workers and the current educational approaches are not fully addressing the need.

State Cyber Security Legislation

The state law 646A.602, 646A.604, 646A.624 has been reviewed to contain data breach with Oregon Administrative Rule 125-800-0005 specifically on State Information Security.

Research Centres and Collaborations

As part of their outreach program on cyber education, Oregon has set up "The Oregon Centre for Cyber Excellence (OCE)". The purpose is to be a national asset to advance substantially the knowledge and educational strategies for cyber-education. They are collaborating with Colleges and Universities in the state. The OCE will establish a core capability in cybersecurity education and research that deploys and integrates the intellectual capacity to deliver a cyber-savvy workforce for both industry and government. The COE will leverage existing consortiums, public-private partnerships, and government working groups to achieve its goals

The General Cyber-Awareness Support (GCS) team that provides the most up to date information and access to cyber-resources across the education spectrum. This team provides a centralized resource for industry and government organizations to leverage as needed when questions on cyber -security arise. The GCS team will be responsible for organizing and executing the quarterly "best-practices" meetings as well as annual state-wide conferences on cyber-security education and training.

The Technology Association of Oregon (TAO) and Oregon University System (OUS) Engineering and Technology Industry Council (ETIC): TAO's mission is to have Oregon be a world-class, multigenerational learning ecosystem that prepares all Oregonians to excel in an inclusive, innovation-based economy. TAO helps the region's technology industry to grow through programs and initiatives that focus on industry promotion, advocacy, professional networks, and innovation. In addition, the TAO Foundation serves as a 501(c) 3 serving as an "umbrella" non-profit to support educational activities and programs that promote wider access to technology education for Oregon K-12 students. TAO membership includes hundreds of technology and technology-enabled companies from start-ups to established industry leaders, service providers, and government, community and educational institutions. Encouragement of Public-Private Partnership.

General Research Focus

The four key research areas are:

1) Improved Internet Privacy and Security

2) Ensuring privacy and security in the Internet of Things

3) Addressing the unique challenges of securing "Big Data" (Privacy and Security)

4) Smart Grid Security and Availability

Oregon State University research focus includes:

1) Detecting insider threats in organizations

2) Diversity & Feedback in Random Testing for Systems Software

3) CAREER: Integrated Automated Software Testing Methods

4) CAREER: Secure Computation

As part of the ongoing assessment of Oregon's needs, the ETIC conducted a cyber-specific education needs assessment in 2013. Three (3) focus areas were:

1) Conducted Market Assessment: To determine cyber-influenced, job functions, titles, certifications and skill requirements required by industry and to evaluate hiring demand trends, and level of cyber-competency demonstrated by current candidates for employment. (Support by Technology Association of Oregon in cooperation with ISACA, AOI, OBA, and Oregon Biosciences Association)

2) Research Assessment: With the support of industry sponsors and the University Deans, ETIC sponsored a round-table discussion to catalog existing cyber-centric research activities, identify synergistic opportunities or research extension to incorporate cyber-centric activity, and qualify the desire and enthusiasm for establishing an Oregon Center for Cyber Excellence.

3) Centre of Excellence Planning and Analysis: Learning from the successful and unsuccessful strategies in other acknowledged Centers of Excellence,

4) Diversity (Students with different background)

Cyber Security Facilities and Working Groups

In conjunction with Industry and other senior Oregon officials, they have set up Project Management Office (PMO). The PMO will help build cross functional teams needed to address the challenges identified Cyber-Needs Assessment. The Program Manager is responsible for project timeline management and tracking, financial management, information technology infrastructure, contracting and legal issues, public affairs, data compliance, technology venturing, and new funding development and administer and facilitate all necessary meetings and reviews required by the effort. The Program Manager and the PMO teams will ensure compliance with all applicable regulations and interface directly with the internal Oregon University System (OUS) leadership, the General Counsel, and other offices as needed.

The PMO and the Program Manager will facilitate meetings with stakeholders and partner organizations to draft, modify, and obtain approval for the initiatives necessary to accomplish the mission of the COE. Under this task the PMO will also seek the input of external experts to assist with the formulation and evaluation of initiatives and outcomes. It is planned that the stakeholders will identify and independent panel to review the overall program bi-annually and provide a comprehensive critique to OUS regarding project progress and relevant recommendations to improve the program. Other teams include:

1) **Cyber-Centric Degree (CCD)**: Charged to focus on using both best practices and innovative new techniques to create more effective cyber-education programs. The team will leverage the partners' existing databases and known activities but will also actively synthesize new cross-cutting opportunities to increase both the

available population of cyber-students but also (importantly) the diversity of those students.

2) **Cyber-Centric Research (CCR)**: Tasked with ensuring the cyber-research in Oregon Universities is supporting both the needs of industry as well as the creating opportunities to train the next generation of cyber-experts. The team will facilitate the initial coordination of the industry partners to include the setting of information, data systems, and operational standards to ensure research conducted in the lab can be easily applied to real-world environments. They will work with each of the University partners initially and on an ongoing basis to help build programs to meet the established standards. At the direction of the industry partners they will seek out interested Oregon researchers to help with specific research needs. They would also assist in having university researchers validate solutions to emerging threats and demonstrate best practices to industry partners as needed. The CCR team would also be chartered to assist in pulling together research experts needed for incident response team needs across the state. This team will include professional staff familiar with a broad swath of cyber-research and industry needs.

3) **General Cyber-Awareness Support (GCS)**: Tasked to provide the most up to date information and access to cyber-resources across the education spectrum. This team provides a centralized resource for industry and government organizations to leverage as needed when questions on cyber security arise. The GCS team will be responsible for organizing and executing the quarterly "best-practices" meetings as well as annual state-wide conferences on cyber-security education and training. The GCS team in conjunction with the CCR team will be responsible for organizing hands-on cyber-security competitions to promote active demonstration of cyber-expertise and critical thinking skills across all levels of students.

4) The GCS team will include educators as well as program coordinators with skills in event planning, digital media outreach, and stakeholder

engagement. They will produce stakeholder reports on the measured progress of the COE compared to the approved plan. The three teams will work seamlessly to ensure the needs of the partners and other Oregon stakeholders are well met.

PENNSYLVANIA

Pennsylvania currently has 7 NSA/DHS-designated academic Centers of Excellence, four of which offer SFS scholarships. Carnegie Mellon University (CMU) is a national leader in cybersecurity research and education and one of the few NSA-designated CAEs in Cyber Operations. Three PA schools were ranked in the top 10 for cybersecurity education by the Ponemon Institute (Carnegie Mellon, U of Pittsburgh, West Chester U). PA also has state government efforts for cybersecurity awareness and response including a CERT team and an ISAC.

State / Policy Activities

PA's Governor has spoken about the importance of public/private partnerships in securing critical infrastructure. PA has some of the nation's leading cybersecurity research centers, most notably at CMU.

Pennsylvania's Information Security Office has a pretty comprehensive website with information for residents about their department, security awareness, and resources:

- http://cybersecurity.state.pa.us/portal/server.pt/community/cyber_security/337

Pennsylvania has an ISAC:

- The Pennsylvania Information Sharing and Analysis Center (PA-ISAC) was established to address the Commonwealth of Pennsylvania's cyber security readiness and critical infrastructure coordination. This initiative is led by the Chief Information Security Officer for the Commonwealth of Pennsylvania's Office for Technology, responsible for leading and coordinating the Commonwealth's efforts regarding cyber readiness and resilience.
- http://www.portal.state.pa.us/portal/server.pt?open=512&objID=504&&PageID=203034&mode=2

Pennsylvania has a CERT team:

- PA-CSIRT, the Commonwealth of Pennsylvania's Computer Incident Response Team
- http://www.depweb.state.pa.us/portal/server.pt/community/pa-csirt/1804

Centers / Facilities

The Software Engineering Institute (SEI) and the CERT Division at Carnegie Mellon University

- http://www.sei.cmu.edu/
    - SEI - A Federally Funded Research and Development Center (FFRDC) sponsored by the U.S. Department of Defense (DoD) and based at Carnegie Mellon University, a global research university annually rated among the best for its programs in computer science and engineering. For four decades, the Software Engineering Institute (SEI) has been helping government and industry organizations to acquire, develop, operate, and sustain software systems that are innovative, affordable, enduring, and trustworthy.
- http://www.cert.org/
    - CERT Coordinating Center - Recognized as a trusted, authoritative organization dedicated to improving the security and resilience of computer systems and networks, the CERT Division is a national asset in the field of cybersecurity. We regularly partner with government, industry, law enforcement, and academia to develop advanced methods and technologies to counter large-scale, sophisticated cyber threats.

CyLab – Carnegie Mellon University

- https://www.cylab.cmu.edu/
- A bold and visionary effort, which establishes public-private partnerships to develop new technologies for measurable, secure, available, trustworthy and sustainable computing and communications systems. CyLab is a world leader in both technological research and the education of professionals in information assurance, security technology, business and policy, as well as security awareness among cyber-citizens of all ages.

The Center for Cyber-Security, Information Privacy, and Trust (AKA The LIONS Center) – Penn State U

- http://ist.psu.edu/future-students/pdf/Cyber-Security.pdf
- http://cybersecurity.ist.psu.edu/
- A research and education center housed at Penn State University. A goal of which is to "play a leading role in helping Penn State pursue security and risk R&D opportunities that revolve around DHS, NSA, and DoD."

Cyber Security Research Alliance

- http://www.arl.army.mil/www/default.cfm?page=1417
- A Collaborative Research Alliance (CRA) led by Pennsylvania State University. The alliance includes The U.S. Army Research Laboratory (ARL), U.S. Army Communications-Electronics Research, Development and Engineering Center, academia and industry researchers to explore the basic foundations of cyber science issues in the context of Army networks. Consortium members also include: Carnegie Mellon University, Indiana University, The University of California at Davis and The University of California Riverside.

SRI Center for Information Management and Cybersecurity

- http://www.sri.com/about/organization/advanced-systems/center-info-management-cybersecurity
- Based in SRI's State College, Pennsylvania and Washington, D.C. locations, manages demanding technology projects requiring high levels of security and restricted access to client data and property.

The Center for Computer Security and Information Assurance – East Stroudsburg University

- http://www.esu.edu/compusec/index.html
- Dedicated to computer security and information assurance education, training, research, literacy, and awareness.

Universities

Carnegie Mellon University

- CAE/IAE, CAE/R
- Also a CAE in Cyber Operations (one of only 13 total schools currently on this list)
- Home of SEI and the CERT Division – two of the most recognized/respected institutions for cybersecurity research and response in the nation.
- The College of Engineering has a notable focus on cybersecurity education and research
    - http://engineering.cmu.edu/companies/strategic_initiatives/cybersecurity.html
- The Information Networking Institute offers a Master of Science in Information Security Technology and Management (MSISTM). Program also has a Cyber Forensics and Incident Response (CyFIR) track.

- o   http://www.ini.cmu.edu/degrees/pgh_msistm/
- CyLab is also located at CMU and they are known for cutting edge security research.

Drexel University

- CAE/IAE
- Cybersecurity Institute and Privacy, Security and Automation Laboratory (PSAL) sites:
    - o   http://drexel.edu/cci/research/institutes/Cybersecurity/
    - o   http://drexel.edu/cci/research/labs/Privacy-Security-Automation-Laborotory/
- The Cybersecurity Institute offers a wealth of professional certification programs, undergraduate degrees, and graduate programs in cyber security, national security, and related specializations.
- From the site: "With a capability for multiple levels of secure and unclassified research, the Drexel Institute leverages a cross-domain and University-wide faculty and staff, world-class research and teaching laboratories and the extensive regional networks immediately accessible to Drexel University located on their main campus in Philadelphia and offices in Washington, D.C. The Institute connects multiple cyber security programs at Drexel, acts as an information repository, provides consultants, conducts applied research and development, and facilitates regional sharing through boundless seminars, workshops and symposia."

East Stroudsburg University of Pennsylvania

- CAE/IAE
- http://www4.esu.edu/about/administration/provost/programs/ccsia.cfm

- Offers an undergraduate program in Computer Security, and specializations in cyber security for both undergraduate and graduate-level computer science majors.

Indiana University of Pennsylvania

- CAE/IAE
- http://www.iup.edu/infosecurity/
- Institute for Information Assurance offers an Information Assurance track through the BS in Computer Science program, as well as a minor in Information Assurance.

Pennsylvania State University

- CAE/IAE, CAE/R
- Penn State offers a number of security options, several of which are through their "World Campus" online college.
- College of Information Sciences and Technology offers a Security and Risk Analysis (SRA) degree: http://ist.psu.edu/future-students/sra
- Online offerings include:
    - Bachelor of Science in Security and Risk Analysis - Information and Cyber Security Option: http://www.worldcampus.psu.edu/degrees-and-certificates/security-and-risk-analysis-bachelors/overview
    - Master of Professional Studies in Information Sciences - Cybersecurity and Information Assurance: http://www.worldcampus.psu.edu/degrees-and-certificates/information-sciences-masters/overview
    - Master of Professional Studies in Homeland Security - Information Security and Forensics Option: http://www.worldcampus.psu.edu/degrees-and-

certificates/homeland-security-information-security-and-forensics/overview

University of Pittsburgh

- CAE/IAE, CAE/R
- http://www.ischool.pitt.edu/ist/index.php
- School of Information Sciences offers an undergraduate Networks and Security specialization and a graduate-level Information Security specialization.

West Chester University of Pennsylvania

- CAE/IAE
- http://www.cs.wcupa.edu/isc/
- The Computer Science Department at WCU has introduced Information Security content such as computer and network security across the undergraduate and graduate curricula through the Information Security Center.

Companies

- The National Cyber-Forensics & Training Alliance
- H-Bar Cyber Solutions
- Wombat Security
- Dell
- Software Engineering Institute at Carnegie Mellon University
- Lockheed Martin
- BAE Systems

Funding

- NSF Scholarship for Service grants awarded to four colleges/universities.

RHODE ISLAND

State / Policy Activities

In July 2011, Representative Jim Langevin (D-RI) announced the establishment of the Rhode Island Cyber Disruption Team (RICDT), whose mission is to prevent and respond to cyber security events and defend the security of critical infrastructure.

The RICDT is comprised of members from the Rhode Island State Police Computer Crimes Unit and individuals representing higher education, hospitals, finance, utilities and defense. This cyber initiative is in line with the President's mandate on cyber security. The following year the state released RI Statewide Cyber Strategic Plan

Law

Rhode Island is one of a minority states - including Massachusetts, California, Connecticut, Oregon, Maryland, and Nevada - have also enacted laws requiring businesses to maintain data security standards to protect state residents' personal information from being compromised.

Centers / Facilities

The University of Rhode Island Digital Forensics and Cyber Security Center (DFCSC) supports state, national, and international public welfare through education, research, training, and service in forensic investigations and securing information systems. The University of Rhode Island and DFCSC are recognized national leaders in providing a strong, cutting-edge, in digital forensics and criminal investigations.

The Pell Center for International Relations and Public Policy, Salve Regina University, Verizon Foundation has awarded a $15,000 grant to the Salve University for International Relations and Public Policy to further the center's efforts in helping to bolster cybersecurity in Rhode Island companies. The grant will support the Rhode Island Corporate

Cybersecurity Initiative which include providing table top exercises for corporate leaders.

Universities

University of Rhode Island is the CAE CAER/ IAE in the state. Salve Regina University, through the Pell Center, has taken a pro-active stance to address cyber security policy preparing corporations to conduct business with an aware cyber leadership stance. The school also has a Homeland Security degree with a concentration in cyber security crime/threat analysis and a Certificate and Graduate Studies in Cybersecurity and Intelligence. URI provided a 2011 Cyber Security Summit.

Companies

- Cybercoders
- The Judge Group
- Corvus Technology Resources
- CVS
- Atrion
- CVS Caremark

- CharterCARE Health Partners
- OSHEAN
- Corvus Technology Resources
- Carousel Industries
- GTECH

Other Notations

RI views itself as being a leader by integrating law enforcement, emergency planners, academics and business to address cybersecurity.

http://www.businessweek.com/ap/financialnews/D9ODLGP81.htm

SOUTH CAROLINA

SC is the poster child for what a state doesn't want to be. Not much was happening in South Carolina until 3.6 million Social Security numbers and 387,000 credit/debit card numbers were compromised in October 2012. In response to the data breach, South Carolina contracted with Deloitte to develop a professional compliance plan. Located on their website, this aggressive assessment program runs 2013/2014 with additional tasks being outlined for the future development of a compliance plan. The State connects to MSISAC and DHS, but nothing original appears to be occurring. Their remains a lackluster approach from the state to embrace a robust cybersecurity posture.

State / Policy Activities

South Carolina instituted cybersecurity stalking, harassment and anti-bullying laws in 2012-13 legislative sessions. The State has awarded Deloitte contracts for incident response. The initial reports – SC needs to establish and mature its cybersecurity profile across the state government and there will be a need for long-term commitment of funding to bring the state up to an acceptable level of performance. As this report was filed in 2014, legislation is in the process of being developed.

Centers / Facilities

South Carolina Information Sharing and Analysis Center (SC-ISAC) is part of the MSISAC network. The website is a good example of check-list compliance with a basic on-line implementation and meeting schedule based upon a contract with Deloitte. This was preceded by the hacking event taking millions of SC Citizen's SSNs and other PII.

Universities

University of South Carolina is a CAE/IAE is a new center with a focus on engineering – specifically securing wired and unwired network and security protocol development for networks and distributed systems.

SOUTH DAKOTA

South Dakota has a generally very low level of activity in cybersecurity; although, there are a number of bright spots that deserve recognition. The state is one of three in the US that has failed to set up data breach notification laws and appears to engage very little in state government cybersecurity promotion, awareness, and education. The state has a small education system but is home to a premier cybersecurity school with Dakota State University. There are no major research centers or companies but two interesting academic research projects mentioned below. In essence, SD is likely in the lower echelon of cybersecurity states but DSU should be further examined for lessons.

State / Policy Activities

South Dakota is one of only three states in the US that has not passed data breach notification laws. There is a very limited cybersecurity web portal provided by the state government that largely offers links to federal resources on information assurance. The state government activity level appears relatively low.

Centers / Facilities

SD is not home to any major research and development centers or national labs focusing on cybersecurity. The research on the subject is largely performed by academics at the schools listed below. For example, at DSU there is the National Center for Information Security and the Center for Information Assurance in Banking and Finance.

Universities

South Dakota has one NSA approved Center of Academic Excellence located at Dakota State University (DSU). DSU offers degrees a master's degree in Information Assurance and Computer Security and bachelor's degree in Cyber Operations. South Dakota State University (SDSU) also offers degree programs in information security. In general the education system in South Dakota is rather small and their offerings are limited compared to larger states. That said, DSU enjoys a strong reputation in the IA industry.

Companies

South Dakota does a have number of cybersecurity employers but appears to have very few large firms that specialize in providing IA hardware, software, or services. The most notable example would be Secure Banking Solutions (SBS). SBS is a security consulting company focusing on finance and banking clients and has strong relationships with the academic centers and researchers mentioned above.

Other Notations

State/Policy Activities

In 2013 the Legislature appropriated $900,000 to fund Dakota State University's information systems programs and cyber security programs. Their cyber security legislation is pending for 2015.

Universities

Dakota State University is the only CAE/IAE in the state South Dakota and received the designation in 2012-13. Their B.X. in Cyber Operations is being augmented with a new doctoral degree in cybersecurity in Fall 2014.

Companies

The need for security professionals companies – SCN Communications, S2Technologies, Stinger Ghaffarian Technologies, Black Hills Corporation.

TENNESSEE

Tennessee has a strong cyber presence due to Oakridge National Laboratory (ORNL) activities, active collaborations with departments of Justice and Homeland Security. Politically, the state doesn't appear to be as engaged on the cyber scene. However, ORNL seems to close a perceived gap at the State level by the depth of the cyber security research and center's focus. The CAE-Rs also have Centers sponsoring summits and workshops.

State / Policy Activities

Tennessee State Government seems to have a limited presence on cybersecurity. The Governor has proclaimed October Cybersecurity Month and the Department of Finance is taking the 'lead' with a 38 page Policy Manual. Tennessee has enacted Cybersecurity Breach Law

Centers / Facilities

Oakridge National Labs has strong mature cybersecurity programs. The Cyber Information Security Research (CISR) linked closely to Departments of Energy and Homeland Security provide multiple internships and fellowship programs. The CISR has sponsored cyber – related workshops annually for the past nine years. ORNL focused cyber topics include defending the network, understanding the threats, securing supply chain and critical infrastructure, and defeating adversaries.

East Tennessee CyberSecurity Summit, a partnership of major players including TVA, ORNL, University of Tennessee - Knoxville, FBI / Department of Justice and Fountainhead College of Technology. This collaboration has provided Summits for seven year, taking a hiatus in 2014.

The University of Memphis Center for Information Assurance has been hosting an Annual Cyber Security Summit since 2007.

Tennessee is a member of the Cyber Security Education Consortium.

Universities

There are one two-year, Jackson State Community College, and three CAE/IAE universities: Fountainhead College of Technology, University of Memphis and University of Tennessee at Chattanooga. University of Memphis is the only research institution. DeVry has campuses in Nashville and Memphis. Tennessee is also part of the

Companies

A number of national companies have a presence in the state:

- Deloitte
- Addeco
- Apex Systems
- Cadre Information Security
- Booz Allen Hamilton
- IBM
- The Hinkle Group

Additional companies working government contracts also include:

- Dynetics
- Hamilton-Ryker
- Unico Technology
- Kensington Solutions
- Babcock & Wilcox
- USEC
- Energy Systems
- Zycron

There is extensive corporate presence buzzing around ORNL and the rest of the state.

TEXAS

This state is VERY invested in cybersecurity. Texas has 16 NSA/DHS-designated Centers of Excellence, four of which offer SFS scholarships. UT San Antonio was ranked as the #1 University for Cybersecurity by HP / Ponemon in 2014. San Antonio has been dubbed "Cyber City USA" due it being the home of the Air Force Cyber Command as well as the National Security Agency's Texas Cryptology Center, a new National Security Agency data center and nearly 80 defense contractors, including dozens focused on information security. Central Texas is clearly one of the major "hot beds" of cybersecurity research and operations in the US with their universities leading the nation in cyber research, the very large presence of federal entities and contractors, and the ever growing private sector cybersecurity firms.

State / Policy Activities

State cyber laws and policies are outline in the "Texas Cybersecurity Framework"

- http://www.dir.state.tx.us/security/policy/Pages/framework.aspx

Bills SB 1102 and SB 1101, passed by the Texas state legislature in 2013, empower the state Chief Information Officer to appoint a coordinator "to oversee cybersecurity matters for this state."

Designated responsibilities for the new role include establishing a council of public and private sector "practitioners" to collaborate on matters of state cybersecurity as well as a voluntary program to recognize "private and public entities functioning with exemplary cybersecurity practices." The Texas Cybersecurity, Education and Economic Development Council (TCEEDC) was created to leverage public/private partnerships to examine the infrastructure of the state's cybersecurity operations with the intent to produce strategies to accelerate the growth of cybersecurity as an industry within Texas, and to encourage industry members to call Texas "home."

- http://www2.dir.state.tx.us/sponsored/SB988/Pages/overview.aspx

Centers / Facilities

The Institute for Cyber Security (ICS) – UT San Antonio (UTSA)

- http://ics.utsa.edu/index.php
- Conducts broad-based, basic and applied scientific research in partnership with academia, government and industry. The institute's researchers include faculty and students from UTSA's colleges of Sciences, Engineering and Business. ICS was established with a competitive $3.5 million grant from the Texas Emerging Technology Fund.

The Center for Education and Research in Information and Infrastructure Security (CERI²S) – UTSA

- http://business.utsa.edu/ceris/index.aspx
- Conducts high impact research in information assurance and security and educates the cybersecurity workforce needed now and in the future. The center's research objective is to offer leading edge solutions that will help to solve cybersecurity problems of national scope and importance.

Center for Information Technology and Cyber Security – Texas A&M San Antonio

- http://www.tamusa.tamus.edu/CITCS/index.html
- Leads the college's cybersecurity education and research efforts

The Center for Information Assurance and Security (CIAS) – Texas A&M College Station

- http://cias.tamu.edu/

- Combines some of the most advanced expertise in the nation to address the broad spectrum of issues involved in the expansion and protection of information and communications infrastructure systems. Offers an IAS lab for education and research.

Center for the Science & Engineering of Cyber Security (CSECS) – Texas Tech

- http://www.depts.ttu.edu/cs/research/csecs/
- The objective of the center is to study principles of Cyber Security, how to measure, assess, and enforce security in legacy systems, and how to build new systems that are secured.

Center for Information Assurance, Statistics, and Quality Control (CIASQC) – Texas A&M Corpus Christi

- The mission of CIASQC is to become the primary South Texas and Gulf of Mexico resource of information assurance, modeling, statistical and quality improvement services, and software engineering for the education, government, health care, and private sectors.

Cyber Security Institute (CSI) – University of Houston

- http://prtl.uhcl.edu/portal/page/portal/SCE/csi
- Collaborates with NASA Johnson Space Center (JSC) and the Bay Area Houston Economic Partnership (BAHEP).

Center for Information and Computer Security (CICS) – University of North Texas

- http://cics.unt.edu/
- An interdisciplinary center, bringing together individuals and organizations with an interest in the areas of information security, computer security, information assurance, and cybercrime.

Center for Identity – UT Austin

- https://identity.utexas.edu/
- The Center for Identity leverages the depth and breadth of expertise throughout The University of Texas at Austin to address the challenge of positively identifying individuals. The Center is organizationally positioned at UT to conduct multi-disciplinary research on all critical facets "identity" – including engineering, science, business, public policy, law, cultural studies, and social studies.

Center for Information Assurance – UT El Paso

- http://www.cs.utep.edu/cfia/
- The mission of the center shall be to promote education and research in information assurance, computer security, and related fields at The University of Texas at El Paso.

Universities

Note: Due to the massive amount of colleges/universities in Texas, this list focuses only on the CAEs – there are even more colleges/universities in Texas that have cybersecurity programs than the ones listed below.

Our Lady of the Lake University

- CAE/IAE
- http://www.ollusa.edu/s/1190/ollu-3-column-noads.aspx?sid=1190&gid=1&pgid=4317
- Offers undergraduate and graduate Computer Information Systems and Security (CISS) degrees that are certified by the National Security Agency (NSA)

Rice University

- CAE/R
- Cybersecurity research is conducted through:
    - The Baker Institute for Public Policy
        - http://bakerinstitute.org/center-for-energy-studies/energy-and-cybersecurity/
- The Computer Security Lab
    - http://seclab.cs.rice.edu/

Richland College of the Dallas County Community College District

- CAE/2Y
- http://www.richlandcollege.edu/forensics/certificates.php
- Offers a digital forensics program and CNSS compliant certificate programs in IA

Southern Methodist University

- CAE/IAE
- http://www.smu.edu/Lyle/Institutes/DeasonInstitute
- The Lyle School of Engineering houses the Darwin Deason Institute for Cyber Security which incorporates a broad, interdisciplinary solution approach and includes faculty, researchers and students from many disciplines within the University, including: Lyle School of Engineering (software, architecture, hardware, protocols, systems engineering), Tower Center for Political Studies (cybersecurity policy, national security), Dedman College of Humanities and Sciences (economics, psychology), Dedman School of Law (cyber law,

forensics), and Cox School of Business (information systems, risk assessment).

Alamo Colleges

- San Antonio College
    - CAE/2Y
    - http://www.alamo.edu/sac/cis/
    - Computer Information Systems program has a security focus and the school offers numerous certificates in digital forensics, information security and assurance.
    - School also offers a Cyber Defenders Camp and houses a lab and private cloud.
- St. Philip's College
    - CAE/2Y
    - Offers Information Security and Assurance AAS degree as well as numerous certification courses geared towards networking, Cisco certifications and CompTIA certifications
        - http://myspccatalog.alamo.edu/preview_program.php?catoid=92&poid=6884&returnto=3652

Texas A&M University (three campuses)

- College Station
    - CAE/IAE, CAE/R
    - http://cias.tamu.edu/education
    - Does not currently offer a degree in Information Assurance and Security. However, does offer options for focus on IA within the departments of Computer Science, Electrical Engineering, and Information Management and

Systems. Majors and minors in IAS as well as Master's and Ph.D. degrees are in various stages of planning and development.
- o Certification Programs in the Departments of Computer Science (College of Engineering) and Information and Management Systems (Mays College of Business) are currently being offered.
- Corpus Christi
    - o CAE/IAE
    - o http://cs.tamucc.edu/
    - o Houses the Center for Information Assurance, Statistics, and Quality Control (CIASQC)
- San Antonio
    - o CAE/IAE
    - o http://www.tamusa.tamus.edu/citcs/computerinformationsystems.html
    - o The Computer Information Systems and Information Assurance and Security programs are run through the Center for Information Technology and Cyber Security

University of Dallas

- CAE/IAE
- The Center for Cybersecurity Education offers an MS in Cybersecurity and an MBA with a concentration in cybersecurity
    - o http://www.udallas.edu/cob/centers/cybersecurity.html

University of Houston

- CAE/IAE

- Offers a Network Management & Security (NMS) certificate and holds Cybersecurity Industry seminars. Various degrees through the School of Science and Computer Engineering offer a security research focus. Hosts the Cyber Security Institute for research and collaboration with NASA Johnson Space Center (JSC) and the Bay Area Houston Economic Partnership (BAHEP).

University of North Texas

- CAE/IAE
- http://cics.unt.edu/education.html
- Offers numerous certifications and an SFS (NSF-funded) PhD program through the Center for Information and Computer Security.

The University of Texas system

- Austin
    - CAE/R
    - https://www.cs.utexas.edu/undergraduate-program/academics/curriculum/degree-plans
    - Houses the Center for Identity and has a fairly large computer science department which offers cybersecurity education and research opportunities. The school's cybersecurity efforts are also spread across a number of colleges and disciplines.
- Dallas
    - CAE/IAE, CAE/R
    - http://www.utdallas.edu/cybersecurity/education/
    - UT Dallas brings together experts from engineering and computer science and colleagues from across campus in fields such as economics, social sciences, criminology,

brain science, management and public policy to help establish broad-based cybersecurity initiatives. Concentrations in cybersecurity are offered through numerous degrees at several colleges.
- o Also houses the Cyber Security Research and Education Institute (CSI)

- El Paso
- CAE/IAE
    - o http://www.cs.utep.edu/
    - o Offers courses and a certificate program in cyber security through the Computer Science department. Also Houses a Center for Information Assurance.
- San Antonio
    - o CAE/IAE, CAE/R
    - o Ranked as the #1 university of cybersecurity
    - o Houses both the Institute for Cyber Security and the Center for Education and Research in Information and Infrastructure Assurance and Security.
    - o The Department of Information Systems & Cyber Security offers a Ph.D. concentration in information technology, an infrastructure assurance concentration as part of the M.S. in information technology, an MBA concentration in infrastructure assurance and a B.B.A. in infrastructure assurance. The Department of Computer Science offers B.S. and M.S. degrees in computer science with concentrations in computer and information security. Additional related coursework is offered through the Department of Electrical & Computer Engineering.

Companies

NOTE: Due to the extreme amount of cyber presence in Texas, the companies/entities listed here mostly pertain to the San Antonio area.

Cybersecurity Companies:

- Digital Defense, Inc.
- KGS
- MDI Security Systems
- NCI
- NewTek
- Rackspace
- SecureInfo Corporation
- SecureLogix Corporation
- ThreatGuard
- Karta Technologies
- Avnet Inc.
- P3s Corporation
- Accenture
- Amer Technology
- Dahill Industries
- Diversified Technical Services
- Computer Sciences Corp
- Sirius Computer Solutions
- General Dynamics C4 Systems
- Raytheon Pikewerks
- Network Security Services

San Antonio "Cyber Highlights"

- The # 2 concentration of data centers in the U.S. (including Microsoft Regional Mega Center).
- Nearly 900 Department of Labor-designated IT companies.
- 80+ companies in the San Antonio Defense Technology Cluster.
- 56,000+ science and technology workforce.
- 20,000 IT-related positions.
- 7,500 SCI-cleared personnel.

- Host of major nationally recognized cyber-related professional events.
- Large Certified Information Systems Security Professionals (CISSPs) workforce.

San Antonio Military (DoD) and Government Cyber Entities:

- NSA / CSS Texas – Texas Cryptologic Center
- Air Force Intelligence, Surveillance and Reconnaissance Agency
- Air Force Electronic Warfare School
- 24th Air Force
- 688th Information Operations Wing
- 67th Network Warfare Wing
- Air Force Cryptologic Systems Group
- Air Force Research Lab
- Defense Information Systems Agency Mega Center
- Navy Information Operations Command Texas
- Joint Reserve Information Operations Center
- Joint Information Operations Warfare Command

Funding

There would be too many grants to find/list so I've just highlighted a couple that I came across.

- NSF Scholarship for Service grants awarded to four colleges/universities
- NSF grant award of $284,000 to The San Antonio College (SAC) Department of Computer Information Systems (CIS) to create an Enhanced Skills Certificate in Server Virtualization to increase the number of technicians who enter the Information Technology

(IT) workforce with competencies in server virtualization and cloud computing.

Other Notations

UTSA Ranked #1 in the nation for cybersecurity in 2014 (HP/Ponemon):

- http://www.computerworld.com/article/2487907/it-skills-training/it-pros-rank-university-of-texas-san-antonio-best-school-for-cybersecurity.html
- http://www.hp.com/hpinfo/newsroom/press_kits/2014/RSAConference2014/Ponemon_2014_Best_Schools_Report.pdf

Texas A&M Engineering Extension (TEEX) service

- Teaches online DHS/FEMA funded training courses in emergency management and cybersecurity, including network security, forensics and more
- http://teex.com/teex.cfm?pageid=NERRTCprog&area=NERRTC&templateid=1856

San Antonio as "Cyber City USA"

- http://www.sanantoniomag.com/SAM/August-2013/Cyber-City-USA/

Central Texas bids to make itself commercial hub of cyber security industry

- http://www.statesman.com/news/technology/central-texas-bids-to-make-itself-commercial-hub-o/nRhhf/

UTAH

Though Utah only has one university that is designated as a CAE, they appear to be growing as a cybersecurity hub. Salt Lake City was named by ClearanceJobs.com as one of the top 5 cities for cybersecurity companies. There is a notable presence of government and contractors in the area, and the NSA recently built their massive data center there.

State / Policy Activities

The only really notable thing I found is the NSA data center. From the NSA: "The Utah Data Center, code-named Bumblehive, is the first Intelligence Community Comprehensive National Cyber-security Initiative (IC CNCI) data center designed to support the Intelligence Community's efforts to monitor, strengthen and protect the nation. Our Utah "mission data repository" is designed to cope with the vast increases in digital data that have accompanied the rise of the global network. The 1.5 billion-dollar one million square-foot Bluffdale / Camp Williams LEED Silver facility houses a 100,000 sq-ft mission critical Tier III data center. The remaining 900,000 SF is used for technical support and administrative space. Our massive twenty building complex also includes water treatment facilities, chiller plants, electric substation, fire pump house, warehouse, vehicle inspection facility, visitor control center, and sixty diesel-fueled emergency standby generators and fuel facility for a 3-day 100% power backup capability."

Centers / Facilities

Space Dynamics Laboratory – Utah State University

- http://www.sdl.usu.edu/capabilities/cyber-security
- A not-for-profit unit of the Utah State University Research Foundation. As a founding member of the Cyber Conflict Research Consortium, SDL works in collaboration with leading

universities and policy research institutions nationwide to support the Department of Homeland Security and military customers with cyber security exercise planning tools and expertise.

Universities

Brigham Young University

- NSA/DHS-designated CAE/IAE (only designated CAE in Utah)
- https://it.et.byu.edu/welcome-information-technology-byu
- IT Program offers a complete Cyber-Security curriculum encompassing Information Assurance and Security, Incident Response & Digital Forensics, Penetration Testing & Ethical Hacking and Secure Systems Administration.
- Has a Cybersecurity Research Lab
    - https://cybersecurity.byu.edu/

Utah Valley University (UVU)

- http://www.uvu.edu/catalog/current/departments/information-systems-and-technology/information-technology-computer-forensics-and-security-emphasis-bs/
- Offers a BS in IT with Computer Forensics and Security emphasis. Also offers a graduate certificate in cybersecurity.

Utah State University

- https://cs.usu.edu/htm/ms-and-mcs-graduate-information/
- Offers cyber security as a focus area within the computer science department.
- Connected to the Space Dynamics Lab which researches cyber security/defense.

University of Utah

- https://continue.utah.edu/edtech/cyber_security
- Offers cybersecurity certification courses for: CompTIA Advanced Security Practitioner (CASP), Certified Ethical Hacker (CEH), and Certified Information Systems Security Professional (CISSP)

Companies

- Raytheon
- FireEye
- AccessData
- Northrop Grumman
- Sedona Technologies
- Blue Coat Systems
- TASC

A lot of defense/Government and contractors are here. Utah also has a gigantic NSA data center that was recently built.

NSA presence:

- http://www.deseretnews.com/article/865578066/NSA-data-center-gives-Utah-cybersecurity-boost.html?pg=all

Salt Lake City named as one of the top 5 cities for cybersecurity jobs:

- http://news.clearancejobs.com/2013/05/23/top-5-cities-for-cyber-security-jobs/
- Salt Lake City has slowly emerged as a technology hub, as well as the home to a growing number of cleared cyber security jobs.

Big data is big business when it comes to cyber security jobs, and perhaps no data center is more famous than the Utah Data Center at Camp Williams in Bluffdale, Utah. The $1.5 billion facility, nicknamed the 'Spy Center,' has the unique mission of aggregating data for the National Security Agency.

The location of the data center was a big win for Utah's tech industry, and is set to be completed in September 2013.

Utah has also developed a corridor of cyber business along the Wasatch Front, located about 50 miles north and south of Salt Lake City. More affectionately referred to as the 'Silicon Slopes,' the area is along the Wasatch Range, midway between the University of Utah and Brigham Young University.

"We have a rich history in defense, IT, and in a lot of other business sectors, as well," said Gary Harter, Executive Director of Veteran's Affairs with the Utah Governor's Office of Economic Development." A number of companies tell us they like coming to Utah, and they like hiring in Utah, because they find good success with employees in Utah who can readily get security clearances."

The state also offers a number of incentives for business, including low energy and utility costs and reasonable permitting and regulation.

Funding

- UVU received a $3 million grant for cybersecurity training from the Department of Labor.

VERMONT

Vermont considers itself a leader in cyber security. The State has a maturity in displaying policies in a well-integrated highly visible approach demonstrating partnerships at multiple levels of government with links to the public and business communities within the state. Their model and websites conveys the message Vermont has a mature cyber security stance at the state, regional and federal levels.

State / Policy Activities

The state markets VT as being a leader in the cyber security realm. The governor has integrated services and policies reflecting a well-integrated approach to communicating with multiple audiences through an easy to use state website: www.itsecurity.vermont.gov. IT policies ranging from 2004 to 2012 have been updated to reflect Vermont's review of 'hot topics' such as Mobile Devices.

Law

Cyber bullying is covered by State Law 16 and passed a Security Breach Notification Law in 2012. The Vermont Law School in 2011 survey assessed cyber vulnerabilities of the US Electrical grid – and found systems at risk.

Centers / Facilities

The Center for Internet Security (CIS), a 501c3 nonprofit organization focused on enhancing the cyber security readiness and response of public and private sector entities, with a commitment to excellence through collaboration. CIS provides resources that help partners achieve security goals through expert guidance and cost-effective solutions.

http://www.cisecurity.org

Universities

Vermont has two centers of academic excellence: Champlain College and Norwich University.

Norwich University's Center for Advanced Computing and Digital Forensics, is working on a project to protect small businesses.

Companies

- Pwnie Express – 2013 raised $5.1 million to test wireless devices and networks in remote locations.
- S2Technologies
- As of 8/20/2014 there were 21 open positions through Indeed for cybersecurity positions related to activities at St. Albans AFB in Vermont.

Other Notations

- http://www.prweb.com/releases/2013/7/prweb10964521.htm

Security Benchmarks

MS-ISAC is well laid out on the Vermont website – readily accessible. While every one of the 50 states is a member, this site leverages its small state reality with connections to New York organizations such as Trusted Purchasing Alliance and Integrated Intelligence Center.

VIRGINIA

State / Policy Activities

Virginia has two distinct security breach disclosure and notification laws that separately cover both personal information and private healthcare related information. The laws are similar to those found in many US states and provide definitions on the types of data to be secured and the mechanisms by which companies must notify victims of a breach. In 2014, Virginia governor Terry McAuliffe created the Virginia Cybersecurity Commission that has been tasked with identifying high risk security threats, promoting cybersecurity awareness and offering expert input related to the security of state networks and information assets. The Commission includes former US Cybersecurity "Czar" Richard A. Clarke. The state appears to still be refining its efforts towards integrating cybersecurity into current disaster recovery planning.

Centers / Facilities

Virginia is home to a huge number of federal agencies that have cybersecurity responsibilities. From the intelligence community there is the CIA, DIA, National Reconnaissance Office, the NGIA, and IARPA. The defense department also has an enormous footprint in Virginia with the very obvious Pentagon but also Army Intelligence & Security Command (INSCOM) and DARPA. The executive branch agencies have to be considered as well despite many of them being headquartered in the District of Columbia. Of particular importance is the DHS with their NCCIC and US CERT in Arlington. Additionally, MITRE Corp has long maintained a large facility in Northern Virginia.

Universities

Virginia has a relatively big university base with many higher education institutions providing cybersecurity curricula and degree specializations.

Both Virginia Tech and the University of Virginia have a number of degree options and multiple academic centers and laboratories devoted to information security topics. The state's inclusion in the beltway has allowed for the development of strong programs at schools like George Washington University, George Mason University, and the many defense and intelligence affiliated schools. The state is home to seven NSA Centers of Academic Excellence and those programs benefit greatly from their relative proximity to the US federal government.

Companies

Multiple large defense contracting firms are either headquartered or have large facilities in Virginia serving the greater beltway area. Firms such as General Dynamics, Lockheed Martin, Boeing, SAIC, L-3 Communications and Booz Allen all provide consulting and contracting services for information security clients throughout both public government and private industry. Virginia's proximity to the federal government attracts large firms in nearly every major economic sector to locate facilities in or around Virginia.

Other Notations

Virginia's unique location allows its institutions and companies to very effectively leverage the many potent funding opportunities that come from the federal government's major grant providing agencies like the DoD, NSF, and Health and Human Services. Also, given the closeness of the Pentagon and State Department along with many intelligence community members there is likely a greater focus on cybersecurity policy, cyber and information warfare strategies, and in general cyber-conflict.

1) Legislation at the state level in the area of cybersecurity.

- Two separate security breach disclosure and notification laws that separately cover personal information and health related information

- Pretty standard with similar components to those in California
- Va. Code § 18.2-186.6, § 32.1-127.1:05
- 2006 audit report finds that nearly all state agencies have security policies and programs but that in general they are inadequate with major failings stemming from confusion regarding who specifically has the organization mandate and authority to monitor information security efforts
- State wide Cybersecurity Commission exists with wide partnerships and representation from industry sectors
    - https://governor.virginia.gov/news/newsarticle?articleId=4817

2) Centers of cybersecurity research/practice.
- Virginia Tech – many cyber related groups, like Cyber Innovation Lab that partners with L-3 Communications, particularly Hume Center for National Security and Technology
- UVA – cybersecurity management program through school of continuing education
- VT - Security and Software Engineering Research Center (S2ERC)
- VT – IT Security Lab
    - Has like 6+ IA related centers
    - And has a SFS program and CAE-E
- Longwood University – Center for Cyber Security (forensically focused)
- GWU
- George Mason
- 7 CAE Institutions

3) Technical/analytical cybersecurity facilities in the state.

- Government/FFRDC
    - Mitre Corp
    - DHS NCCIC & US CERT
    - Pentagon (DoD)
    - DARPA/IARPA
    - Army INSCOM
    - National Reconnaissance Office / National Geo-spatial Intelligence Agency
    - CIA, DIA, etc.
- Private Sector
    - Defense Industry Companies
        - General Dynamics, L-3, Lockheed, et al
    - Huge contractor presence (Boeing, SAIC, GD)

4) What are the state's cybersecurity main research/practice focus(es).

- National security, cyberwarfare, software engineering, management and leadership, intelligence and analytics, etc.

5) What funding do they have from the funding agencies (NSF, etc.)

- Massive funding…given proximity to DoD, NSF, NASA, etc

WASHINGTON

While Washington has yet to do a focused messaging campaign, the state has a highly collaborative landscape of cybersecurity activities occurring around the state. The state has been building a strong profile to address critical infrastructure issues related to a variety of resources with a strong concentration in the electrical grid and Emergency Preparedness. At the same time, different sectors including government, military, private, public and academia interact consistently in formal and informal settings. Washington has a strong informal network of cyber and information security professionals through Agora, which, for the past twenty years has convened quarterly to stay abreast of the latest information within the field. This stealth organization is representative of the Washington State Cybersecurity milieu. Innovation happens in Washington – and events often fly below the radar.

Tacoma and Pierce County have proclaimed leadership as a stream of economic development for the South Puget Sound to serve as a driver for cybersecurity within the state. The Washington National Air and Army Guard have cyber security units and a strong reputation for the work being accomplished internally and their ability to work with other sectors within the state and Canada. However, Seattle and the East Side, Bellevue, Kirkland, Redmond support strong cyber security business climates.

State / Policy Activities

Washington State enacted an anti-cyber-stalking group early on. The legislature has enacted cyberbullying legislation and there is pending legislation in HB 1365-2013-14 requiring cities and counties to provide higher levels of security for their courts. State has recently brought on a consultant, former CISO of Seattle to ramp up a cohesive state policy. Washington State is active in the MRSC and has a strong relationship with the Department of Homeland Security (via PRISEM). Individual organizations provide a prominence to the state. Association of Washington Cities promotes cyber security across the state.

Centers / Facilities

Pacific Northwest National Labs

Headquartered in Richland, WA, PNNL maintains offices in Seattle and concentrates cybersecurity research in several areas. Their Electricity Infrastructure Operating Center (EIOC) focuses on protecting the cyber-based systems that monitor and control our nation's critical infrastructure with an emphasis on Operating Environments & Policy/Education and Training. PNNL leverages a Regional approach by partnering with Gonzaga University, University of Washington, Washington State University and University of Wyoming, Montana Tech – The University of Montana.

UW Center for Information Assurance Cybersecurity

Affiliated with the University of Washington is a CAE/R and has been involved in Cyber security events since 2008. The CIAC umbrellas the University of Hawaii and has provided talks, supported conferences and assorted venues annually on cybersecurity topics.

Center for Regional Disaster Resilience

Center for Regional Disaster Resilience has conducted the second annual Emerald Downs Cyber Summit, preparing for the third event. This one day event convenes multiple sectors, public, private, government, military, non-profit, to address cyber security issues in concert with Emergency Disaster/First Responders.

UWT's South Sound Technology Conference

UWT's South Sound Technology Conference for the past decade has been providing a one day forum on relevant technology topics. Cybersecurity has been featured prominently as the City of Tacoma and Pierce County jockey for position as a cyber hub. **PRISEM**: Public Regional Systems Event Management – a DHS funded project in its fifth year has established a collaboration among 15 entities including cities, ports and counties to provide a warning alert system to monitor cyber attack activity against the infrastructure maintained by these organizations. PRISEM, in collaboration with WA State Dept. of Commerce, has received funding to transition to a non-profit business model.

On-line Trust Alliance

Non-profit- dedicated to raising the bar on cybersecurity

WSU

Since 2011 WSU has provided an annual two day conference in Emergency Preparedness with a nod to the role of technology and social media and on-going critical infrastructure maintenance.

Universities

The University of Washington is a CAE/R utilizing three campuses and the UW Professional Continuing Education organization to offer an Information Security Risk Management Certificate with an assortment of technology/security focused certificates. UWT is one of six universities nationally combining business and cybersecurity to develop leaders for the rapidly expanding cyber workforce. UWB is focused on a cybersecurity engineering degree and the main campus, through the I-School, provides a cybertrack within the MSIM program. The community college/technical college system has schools offering two year applied degrees, transfer programs to 4 year institutions and some community colleges are moving to offer four ear degrees. These schools include: Spokane Falls, Edmonds CC, Olympic College, Green River CC, Clover Park Technical CC, Whatcom Community College (CAE/2Y)and Highline Community College (a pending CAE/2Y). In 2007 Washington State University's College of Electrical Engineering and Computer Science received a grant to work on critical electrical grid infrastructure. Within the Washington State Community College System, a variety of institutions are addressing cybersecurity education/training. Schools and districts within

Washington's K-12 system are adding technology courses with offerings for cybersecurity opportunities.

Several private institutions, in addition to DeVry, City University in Seattle, Seattle University and a satellite campus of Northeastern University are providing cyber security degrees or concentrations in the subject.

Companies

Washington State is the home of MicroSoft, Amazon, Starbucks, Boeing; companies with high cyber security needs. Google has developed a presence and IBM, Booz Hamilton, Deloitte and a myriad of government focused contractors are attracted to JBLM, Fairchild AFB, Bangor Naval Base/Bremerton Shipyard. Additional companies include Coalfire Systems, Internet Identity, Morpho, Puget Sound Energy, Praxair Puget Sound Energy, Distributions, Inc., Seattle Public Utilities, Tacoma Public Utilities, Snohomish Public Utilities, SunGard, Verizon Wireless, T-Mobile, Witt Associates, WSEMA, Washington State Emergency Management Division, Bonneville Power, and the list goes on. The Agora estimates a network of between 1200 to 1500 – and these professionals are employed throughout Washington and the Pacific NW (some attend from Canada and D.C.). Cyberpath is located in the TriCities.

Other Notations

1) http://education-portal.com/cyber_security_career_training_in_washington.html

2) 2005 NSF Grant David Bakken, School of Electrical Engineering and Computer Science, 509/335-2399, bakken@wsu.edu
Robert Strenge, WSU News Services, 509/335-3583, rstrenge@wsu.edu

3) Gonzaga University, Montana Tech - The University of Montana, University of Washington, University of Wyoming, , Washington State University

4) http://www.snopud.com/Site/Content/Documents/cyber/CyberSummit414-Agenda.pdf

5) http://knowledgecenter.csg.org/kc/system/files/burnett_2012_table_a.pdf

WEST VIRGINIA

West Virginia has two CAEs and has received some recognition for their risk management initiatives at the state level. A 2012 Deloitte-NASCIO Cybersecurity Study highlights West Virginia as a leading practice for their risk management strategy (more information on this is in the next section).

State / Policy Activities

West Virginia's Office of Technology Cyber Security Program won an award in 2011 for Risk Management Initiatives.

- http://www.nascio.org/awards/2011awards/riskmgmt.cfm

"In West Virginia, a combination of legislation and an Executive Order helped to define and require the development of Executive-wide policy, training, audit for compliance, and mitigation of vulnerabilities. In addition, Executive Order 6-06 called for the formation of an Executive Branch Information Security Team and a Privacy Management Team. The Governor's Executive Information Security Team (GEIST) was subsequently established which enlisted high-level departmental operatives to extend the reach of the Office of Information Security and Controls. An Information Security Strategic Plan was developed and, over time, resources and tools have been acquired to focus on the information and cybersecurity challenge of overall risk reduction through strong controls and heightened awareness. In addition, an audit function was established at the Office of Technology; the Office of Technology will have a base audit that can satisfy requirements of multiple audits conducted throughout the year, saving significant time for repeated audits on the same control set."

- http://www.deloitte.com/assets/Dcom-UnitedStates/Local%20Assets/Documents/AERS/us_aers_nascio%20Cybersecurity%20Study_10192012.pdf

Centers / Facilities

Center for Identification Technology Research (CITeR) – WVU

- http://www.citer.wvu.edu/
- CITeR is a National Science Foundation (NSF) Industry/University Cooperative Research Center (I/UCRC)

Institute for Information Assurance Studies (IIAS) – WVU

- http://www.csee.wvu.edu/IIAS/
- Housed in the Lane Department of Computer Science & Electrical Engineering

Universities

Blue Ridge Community and Technical College

- CAE/2Y
- http://catalog.blueridgectc.edu/preview_program.php?catoid=3&poid=173&returnto=65
- Offers a Cyber Security A.A.S. and a number of professional certifications in IT/security

West Virginia University

- CAE/IAE, CAE/R
- http://www.csee.wvu.edu/IIAS/education.html
- Offers a variety of IA programs including: Biometric Systems at the Undergraduate Level, a Computer Forensics graduate certificate, and an Information Assurance and Biometrics graduate certificate.

- Also houses the Institute for Information Assurance Studies and CITeR

Companies

- Lockheed Martin
- TASC
- SecureStrux LLC
- FireEye
- Mitre Corporation
- Criterion Systems

Funding

None found

WISCONSIN

There are currently no NSA/DHS designated CAEs in the state, though the University of Wisconsin system does have some programs, centers, and focus on cybersecurity. Annual Cyber Security Summits have been held the last two years at different colleges in the state (Waukesha County Technical College and Marquette University). Researchers at UW-Madison received a portion of a large federal grant for developing secure software for infrastructure systems.

State / Policy Activities

The state has a "Ready Wisconsin" site, part of WI's emergency management efforts and in line with DHS's "Ready" campaign, promotes cybersecurity awareness and safety tips and links for citizens. There is also a state Bureau of Security.

Centers / Facilities

Wisconsin Information Security Center (WISC)

- Part of the Wisconsin Security Research Consortium (WSRC), a government contractor
- Mission is to "accelerate the growth of a high-tech/knowledge-based workforce with capabilities to provide solutions to problems of national security importance. It will build upon the region's economic diversity by promoting cybersecurity research, education and technology innovation. WSRC will foster collaborative and strategic alliances between government agencies, private industry and academic institutions."
- http://universityresearchpark.org/the-property/wisc/

Center for Cryptography, Computer and Network Security – UW Milwaukee

- The center's purpose is the advancement of knowledge in the areas of cryptography, computer security, network security and related areas from a theoretical as well as a practical viewpoint.
- This center is the focal point of collaborative efforts to strengthen cyber security education through the UWisc system
- http://webdev.cae.uwm.edu/ceas/faculty_research/research_centers/cryptography_computer_and_network_security/

Morgridge Institute for Research – UW Madison

- Not a particularly cyber-focused facility, but they were recently awarded a large national grant in collaboration with Indiana University and the University of Illinois at Urbana-Champaign in order to research strengthening/security software for critical infrastructure.
- http://discovery.wisc.edu/morgridge/

Universities

The University of Wisconsin system

- Parkside
    - Offers a Cyber Security certificate program that meets the National Security Systems National Training standards.
    - http://www.uwp.edu/learn/programs/cybersecurity.cfm
- Stout (Polytechnic)
    - Offers an Information Assurance and Cyber Security Concentration within their B.S. in Applied Mathematics and Computer Science.

- o   http://www.uwstout.edu/programs/bsamcs/conc-iacs.cfm
- Milwaukee
    - o   Hosts the Center for Cryptography, Computer and Network Security within the College of Engineering and Applied Science
    - o   Computer science program offers data security concentration
    - o   http://webdev.cae.uwm.edu/ceas/academics/
- Other
    - o   Both UW-Madison and Eau Claire locations also offer some cybersecurity courses in their computer science departments but don't really seem to have a heavy focus on security

Waukesha County Technical College – Pewaukee

- Offers three technical certifications in IA areas including: Cyber Security Specialist, Security Administrator, and Risk Management
- 2014 Cyber Security Summit was held here
- http://www.wctc.edu/index.php

Companies

- Wisconsin Security Research Consortium
- USIS

Funding

- Collaborative Research grant from the NSF for Wisconsin Collaborating Campuses on Cyber Security.

- $23.6 million grant awarded to a group of research institutions, including UW-Madison, as part of a Broad Agency Announcement (BAA 11-02) by the U.S. Department of Homeland Security Science and Technology Directorate to address threats arising from the development process of software used in technology ranging from the national power grid to medical devices.
    - http://www.news.wisc.edu/21224

WYOMING

Governor Mead has been pushing for betting Internet access in the state of Wyoming. The governor is aware of cybersecurity issues and the state government website provides helpful links for information/awareness. No schools in WY have designations as CAEs, and only one that I found has a cybersecurity program.

State / Policy Activities

Nothing that stands out. They have pretty standard Electronic Crime statues which can be read here:

http://www.forwardedge2.com/pdf/WY-laws.pdf

Centers / Facilities

NCAR-Wyoming Supercomputing Center (NWSC)

- Not particularly cybersecurity related, but the only real cyber facility in the state that I found
- "Provides advanced computing services to scientists studying a broad range of disciplines, including weather, climate, oceanography, air pollution, space weather, computational science, energy production, and carbon sequestration. It also houses a landmark data storage and archival facility that will hold, among other scientific data, unique historical climate records."

Universities

Sheridan College (Northern Wyoming Community College District)

- Offers an AAS degree in Cyber Security

- "Sheridan College is the first in the state to offer a degree in Cyber Security. The Cyber Security program serves as the foundation for a baccalaureate program for those who wish to transfer, as well as direct job entry skills for those not pursuing a baccalaureate program."
- http://www.sheridan.edu/site/sc/academics/programs-and-majors/cyber-security/

Companies

- Green House Data

Funding

None found

Made in the USA
Middletown, DE
01 September 2022